The Financially Confident Woman

You can't pay your credit card bill with a credit card and other habits of

The Financially Confident Woman

Mary Hunt
Publisher of *Cheapskate Monthly*™

Broadman & Holman Publishers
Nashville, Tennessee

Published by Broadman & Holman Publishers, Nashville, Tennessee
Acquisitions & Development Editor: Vicki Crumpton
Interior Design: Steven Boyd
Printed in the United States of America

4262-85

Dewey Decimal Classification: 332.024
Subject Heading: PERSONAL FINANCE / MONEY
Library of Congress Card Catalog Number: 96-3422

Published in association with the literary agency of Alive Communications, Inc., 1465 Kelly Johnson Blvd., Suite 320, Colorado Springs, CO 80920

ISBN 1-56865-612-2

For Harold,
the most patient man on earth

Contents

Nine Habits of the Financially Confident Woman

Becoming a Financially Confident Woman

Acknowledgments

Love and support are a couple of things of which I am particularly fond. For giving them to me, I wish to thank manager Cathy Hollenbeck and all the staff at *Cheapskate Monthly;* my Friday night support group, Paul and Jan Sandberg and Mark and Rosalie Copeland; my Monday night care and share group; my editor, Vicki Crumpton; agent, Greg Johnson; and last and most importantly, my husband, Harold, and wonderful sons, Jeremy and Josh. I could never do this without all of you.

Introduction

Hi there, and welcome to my book. I'm not only pleased you're reading this introduction; I'm approaching ecstasy because it means I'm right!

Experts think we don't read introductions. I find that hard to believe because I *always* read the introduction, and the dedication, and everything else preliminary. In fact, I read the copyright page and all the Library of Congress cataloging information. I hoped and prayed that someone who thinks like me would pick this book up; and sure enough, here you are, the answer to my prayer.

If this were a book of fables or even a novel of some sort, I'm quite certain it would have come together a bit more quickly. But writing about myself, my failures and struggles with money, and my outrageous abuse of credit cards is very humbling if not downright terrifying. What will you think about me once you find out what I'm really like? Will you understand that I'm in process, that I'm still tempted by preapproved credit card applications and compulsive overspending? How can God possibly use me to help others become more financially responsible when I have so much more to learn myself? Will you say I don't look anything like my picture?

And so during these many moments of conviction when the words just wouldn't flow, I found myself reaching for the bottle of lotion I keep on my desk. Call me hyperactive, but I have a very difficult time just sitting and doing nothing. The moisturizing ritual became an act so frequently repeated it became almost automatic, something that will mean a great deal more to you once you've read chapter 5.

I hope you like my book, that it entertains you and confirms for you that no matter how crazy you've been with money I've got you beat. I hope it makes you confident that with God's power you can change, makes you excited about the future, makes you stop throwing away your bank statements, and gives you confidence you can become the title. Or at the very least it makes you not regret you bought it.

My journey into the credit card abyss began quite innocently. I would never have considered my behavior irresponsible. I was simply agreeing to have it all now and pay for it later. I was pushing the envelope, living on the edge, going for the gusto because I would only go around once (obviously every marketing genius dreams of consumers like me). Throwing caution to the wind and living spontaneously were my definitions of enjoying life.

Me irresponsible? No way! I was progressive, inventive, and creative. The challenge was that in order to carry off this persona I needed money—lots of it, and more than I happened to have at the time. I was driven to find new and better ways to mortgage my future; otherwise, I might be forced to stifle my marvelously whimsical tendencies and sudden inspirations.

I learned the hard way that irresponsible financial behavior eventually brings financial devastation. Activities meant to make me soar clipped my wings instead and sent me hurling into a pit of despair. My plan for freedom became my own prescription for bondage.

Financially irresponsible people are not bad people. They've simply fallen prey to *bad habits.* They often don't know when they're making mistakes; therefore, they don't learn from them until it's too late. The good news is bad habits can be unlearned and good habits learned. *Having a desire to change is the key to becoming financially responsible*.

If you are searching for quick fixes or ways to manipulate your present situation to qualify for more debt, this may not be the book for you. However, if you're tired of always being broke, feel you cannot handle another monthly bill, are fresh out of juggling techniques, and fear things might never change, I'm glad we've found each other.

This is not a book about budgets. Instead it is a book about how to identify irresponsible and negative financial behaviors and change them forever.

This is not a book about how to get more money. More is never enough. It's a book about how to become financially confident by learning how to manage what you already have. It's not a book equating poverty with spirituality. It is a book about right living, abundance, joy, and the peace of mind that results from living a life that is pleasing to God.

In encouraging you to look deep into your personal belief system, I've had to come to a screeching halt on more than one occasion and search my own heart, that secret place deep within from which come my own attitudes and values. It continues to be a humbling experience to realize that only as I'm willing to change myself can I help others do the same.

I have so much to tell you, and I pray it will change your life the way it has mine. No matter where you are on the spectrum of financial responsibility, I have something wonderful to offer you—hope, confidence, and peace. God's peace.

PART ONE

Self-Examination

ONE

Confessions of a Financially Irresponsible Woman

When money talks it often merely says "goodbye."

POOR RICHARD JR.'S ALMANAC (1906)

I received my first taste of what I thought was freedom when I left home to attend college in California. I'll never forget my first week in Los Angeles. Like my first kiss, it was better than I'd ever imagined; and quite frankly, I wished it could last forever. The beautiful weather, the palm trees, the lights, and the excitement of the big city were far beyond anything I'd ever imagined during my numerous dreaming sessions. I just knew that college would be my paradise on Earth.

I intended to waste no time fulfilling my childhood promise: When I grew up I'd be rich. You see, I mistakenly equated my terminal sadness with the fact that I felt poor. It made perfect sense to me then that being rich would produce happiness, and I just couldn't wait to be happy.

As California's newest Cinderella, I had been planning this transition from poor to rich for a long time. The moment I set foot on campus, my dream ceased being a fantasy and became a self-fulfilling prophecy.

I wasted no time opening a checking account. I knew I would need one to handle my financial activities. I was quite unfamiliar with this grown-up device that came without owner's manual or instructions. Quite frankly, I didn't think much about it because it appeared so simple, so user-friendly.

I saw my checkbook as a security measure that would ensure my money was safe in the bank in the event of an untimely mugging or careless misplacement. I believed the legendary admonition that it's just not safe to carry cash. I had no ulterior motives in getting this handy-dandy accessory, but I didn't know my checkbook carried a hidden danger.

The first time the idea crept into my mind I was with a group of friends—friends with cars and freeway savvy who introduced me to the world of California shopping malls. The idea of writing checks with no money in the account was about as insane an idea as I'd ever had. I half-heartedly pushed it out of the way. Seconds later the idea returned. The more I thought about it the less outrageous it seemed. After all, who'd know? No one, not even the sales clerk could know exactly how much money I had in my account. I could buy the things I wanted and, as a bonus, impress my friends with my fiscal prowess. Given sufficient time to get used to the concept—about thirty seconds—my idea didn't seem so insane after all. I'd do it just this once.

Unfortunately, my crazy idea worked quite well. Not only were my friends impressed with my ability to keep up with them (they didn't come right out and say it, but I knew), the salesperson had to have been surprised by my ability to buy whatever I wanted. Acting rich gave me a sense of significance and, in turn, a fabulous feeling.

I figured out how to shop on Wednesday, get paid from my college library job on Friday, deposit the check on Monday and have time to spare to cover the checks I'd been writing all week long. Nobody was harmed because no one knew the difference. It was exciting, too, because it felt like I was getting away with something—beating the system. Taking this kind of risk was exhilarating in some crazy way.

I didn't see what I was doing as wrong; I was simply being creative in my efforts to keep up the style to which I was becoming increasingly accustomed. Even when I bounced checks I didn't question the procedure I'd discovered. I was pretty easy on myself, concluding I wasn't exactly overdrawn, just under-deposited.

My checking account escapades were the start of a terrible destructive habit I allowed to take root in my life: I habitually engaged in the activity of acquiring first and figuring out how to pay later.

Somehow I made it through college without being subjected to public humiliation for having accounts closed due to excessive overdrafts, and I escaped being arrested for kiting (the illegal practice of writing a bad check on one account to cover an overdraft on another). I have no idea how much money I spent covering "insufficient funds" fees, but it had to have been a lot. Still, I refused to see my financial behavior as irresponsible or self-destructive. After all, like many college students, I'd just spent the better part of four years financially strapped. My creativity allowed me to spend what I didn't have at the moment to get what I couldn't live without. It was no big deal, and I didn't plan to do it forever.

When I married Harold shortly after graduation, I just assumed that I'd never have to worry about money again. After all, a man is supposed to take care of his wife, handle the finances, and make sure she, whose job it is to spend the money, has plenty of it. In the absence of any counseling to the contrary, I figured that's the way it would be. However in hindsight, the fact that I insisted we needed a credit card (just in case of emergency, of course) is clear evidence that deep inside I didn't feel he could handle his financial responsibilities and needed my intervention.

Plastic Significance

The arrival of my first credit card triggered another insane idea in my head. I found that a gasoline credit card was far superior to my checkbook. It was easier to use at the corner gasoline station. But the idea that went off in my head was far more dangerous than mere convenience. It shouted, "We get free gas whenever we want it!" Not having to worry about whether I had enough cash to pay for gasoline and choosing "full serve" to boot made me feel rich, dignified, and significant. My contact with rich people had been limited, so the way they behaved was pretty much left up to my imagination. And I had one terrific imagination!

As a young girl I was blessed with a best friend, Judy. As a bonus to our friendship, Judy's parents were the richest people I'd ever known. They had a beautiful home and contemporary furnishings. Judy's dad had a telephone in his car, and her mom owned a successful business. Judy had what I understood to be unlimited access to her mother's accounts at all kinds of stores, not the least of which was the little corner grocery store. Whenever I stayed over at Judy's—which was as often as I could finagle parental permission—I, too, became a rich kid. I was treated with the same privilege, love, and respect as a member of the Ellis family. I had acceptance and approval.

Judy and I had great freedom, which included unlimited entitlement to the little, corner grocery store. We could buy anything we wanted anytime we felt like it. Anything. And we never needed money. The store owner, Rawley, made us feel like the most important girls in the world; and armed with Judy's signature alone, we could be on our way with the best selection of groceries any two teenagers could ever imagine. There were no limitations and no accountability—at least that was my perception. I wonder now what kind of conversations resulted when Mrs. Ellis received that monthly bill. But for me that part of the story didn't exist. I'm sure I just assumed that because they were rich, eventual payment was just taken care of—the same way a princess is taken care of. It just happens.

I lived for the weekends I would be able once again to experience firsthand the delights and freedom of being rich. To this day some of my fondest memories involve stayovers at Judy's house, where I received my first taste of significance and individual importance. It's no wonder I associated those wonderful feelings with money.

As you might imagine, the initial excitement of that new gasoline entitlement wore off quickly when the monthly statement arrived. Surely someone had made a mistake. There's no way we'd filled up that many times. And the worst part? The gasoline company wanted full payment immediately. It was clear to me that we needed another brand of gasoline credit card to spread the purchases around. Then another and another.

One day while I strolled through a local department store, a salesperson invited me to apply for the store's credit card. All I needed to qualify was a valid credit card, and my gasoline card would do. Talk about too good to be true! Of course I accepted with no regrets because once again I felt I was doing something noble—preparing for emergencies. Within just a few minutes I was entitled to lots more than only gasoline. This revolving credit idea was really getting into my blood. It seemed so workable, so logical. A two hundred dollar purchase wasn't that at all. It was merely a ten-dollar monthly payment. Highly affordable in my book. Of course intellectually I'm sure I knew better, but my ability to slip into denial transcended reason. I was able to remain comfortable because of my unique ability to justify and defend my activities.

My Plastic Safety Net

It didn't take long for me to get caught up in the excitement of credit card acquisitions. I was like a kid working on a baseball card collection. I never intended to really use them but to have these lines of credit all in place in case of emergencies. To me they were like seat belts, a first aid kit, jumper cables, and oat bran all rolled into one neat little package. I was convinced of their ability to protect, nourish, comfort, and cure.

I had many "emergencies" over the following years and felt fully entitled to meet those needs using our credit cards. What I believed about them was absolutely true. They worked like a charm to relieve pain and worry. They offered asylum from the penalties of past-due property taxes and provided wonderful Christmas holidays for our two boys and extended families. Even the dentist and preschool accepted plastic. Credit cards worked perfectly in bridging the gap between what I'd determined was our woefully inadequate income and the cost of maintaining the minimum acceptable lifestyle, a lifestyle which demanded I provide for our two little boys, Jeremy and Josh, all the things I'd missed during my childhood.

Just when I thought it couldn't get any better, several of our credit cards offered that glorious added feature—the cash advance. Even though plastic was accepted nearly everywhere, there were occasions when I needed plain old green stuff, and the cash advance was right there to the rescue.

Because we kept up with the monthly payments and incurred a minimal number of late fees, we were fairly well qualified to land new forms of credit. I knew how the applications needed to read in order to be approved.

Because our credit report was pretty clean and Harold had an excellent job with a large California bank, we were able to purchase a home in a location where home values were escalating at an unprecedented rate. Our home in Orange County was increasing in value by at least 20 percent a year. At this rate our three-bedroom house would be worth $5 or even $10 million by the time we wanted to think about retirement. There was no need to start a savings program or plan for the future. When the time came, we'd put out a For Sale sign, sell the house quickly, gather up our millions, and sail off into retirement heaven.

Because I'd gotten into the habit of always spending more money than we had available, on quite a few occasions we had to refinance and take out second and even third mortgages on the house. After all, we had to eat. And with each new loan came another payment and greater necessity to find new sources of income. Of course, each time we refinanced I promised Harold that we'd pay off the debts and stop using credit as soon as we got things straightened out or this thing or that thing happened.

But it never straightened out—for a million reasons, not the least of which was because we were young and figured we'd have plenty of time to save when our income increased. As the years passed, it was our financial obligations that increased.

Meltdown

After we'd been married for about twelve years, the minimum monthly payments on all our debts were totaling an amount dangerously close to our take-home pay. Most of our credit card credit lines were at the max, and juggling became a way of life. It was not unusual for us to use next month's check to cover this month's bills, or pay half the bills this month and half next. We were constantly chasing new forms of credit only to stay afloat.

I convinced my banker husband that his occupation would never cut it income wise and that we should consider self-employment. It seemed like a good idea to me. Self-employed people, so I thought, were smart and wealthy. Self-employment would allow us to make the amount of money we needed. Harold wasn't all that enamored with the future the bank seemed to be offering and detested the politics he was being pressured to play. The banking industry was facing major revamping, and the idea of a new challenge and the bright hope of self-employment became attractive to both of us. We had dreams to fulfill and children to raise. We wanted a bright and inviting future, not one plagued with a constant shortage of money.

Once we opened our minds to such a drastic employment change, we became a couple of giant magnets to the many seeming opportunities that existed. Harold had befriended a couple of his bank clients, and both of us couldn't help but be fascinated by their new German-made sports cars and very large, daily cash deposits. We were entertained in their Newport Beach, California, homes, and their lifestyles really turned our heads. It didn't take long for their casual interest in us to become more deliberate. We were being sought after to join them in their mega-enterprise. They didn't pressure us. They simply befriended us and allowed us to view the good life. We checked the organization out as well as we could;

however, our minds were already made up. I'm sure we were blind to warning signs that must have been screaming out to us.

We went to Atlanta as honored guests at the organization's annual sales meeting. Imagine how significant we felt as our friends who had made their way high into the organization introduced the banker who'd caught this marvelous organization's vision and was leaving sixteen years of tenure to become the newest company owner.

As thousands of people cheered, the entire episode was videotaped. I remember thinking how wonderful it was to have this momentous occasion recorded for our family's history and generations to come. I could see myself slipping behind the steering wheel of my own German-made sports car. I was so proud, so optimistic, and so happy for my husband who'd finally made a very difficult decision to leave his comfort zone and take an exciting risk.

Our trip back to California was energized by our resolve to be excellent employers and worthy stewards of this magnanimous new wealth that was about to be thrust upon us. Our plans were set and we wasted no time putting them into action.

Harold gave his resignation and customary notice to the bank, and we figured out how we would borrow the thousands of dollars we'd need to get into the business. A short-term loan was all we needed because this particular business was cash intensive. Repayment would be swift and sure.

Of course we needed a site for the business. (Did I mention it involved reselling poor quality merchandise? I mean very poor quality—so awful, in fact, this stuff would hardly have a chance of moving at a garage sale.) Since I'd dabbled in industrial real estate, I was able to pull off a lease and even earned a commission. Next we needed to furnish the place. We rented rooms full of office furnishings and accessories. One tenet of corporate headquarters was that each franchise needed to have a look of success to attract the caliber of people who would make sure that success continued.

We worked hard, but it was clear almost from the start that we'd been terribly misled about how easy it was going to be to get up and running profitably in a short time. Every cent we had borrowed plus every additional dollar we could rake off our credit card limits was poured into the business. We felt we'd already put so much in we had to protect the initial investment. We justified letting our personal bills slide for a few months because we were still convinced the cash would start flowing. Then we'd get everything caught up and be none the worse for the temporary delay.

About two months into this self-employment nightmare I grew fearful. The honeymoon was over and the tension was setting in. We weren't able to hire all the people we needed in spite of very expensive advertising. Our furniture and warehouse rental payments were much larger than they seemed when we signed the paperwork. It was clear we were undercapitalized and overly optimistic.

And those two wonderful men who'd introduced us to our dream of a lifetime? They were gone and have remained gone to this day. Clearly their automobiles and homes were rented short-term to allow them to come into the area, fleece every sucker they could find, and leave before anyone could catch up with them. They were clever too. We had nothing with which we could prove fraud or deception.

Four months from start to finish. The longest four months of our lives. We experienced every emotion of which we were capable, usually all at once. As our hopes and dreams were being dashed so was our relationship. Things hadn't been really terrific between us for quite a long time before this self-employment episode; but we passed that off as the financial strain we were under, my unwillingness to spend less, and insistence that he earn more. This new dream business had given us a common goal, and it temporarily rekindled our marriage

It took four months for our dream to die. We buried it the day all the rented furniture was repossessed and we walked away from the building. It was a painful and torturous death, and with it something in both of us died. Harold had gone from tenured bank employee to future millionaire to unemployed business owner in about sixteen weeks. To make matters worse, he had no unemployment benefits. Our income was zero, our home was moving closer to foreclosure each day, and we were defenseless against the pit of despair into which we were slipping. We had no idea what to do. When we needed each other the most, we were the least able to communicate or to even reach out to each other. We were two angry individuals completely isolated in our pain.

I cannot remember a time before or since that I have ever felt such utter defeat, pain, anger, and debilitating fear. When faced with life's challenges I had always had a plan B, another idea, an alternative. My controlling temperament had always pulled through, but I was completely unable to rescue this situation. We had bills on top of bills, debts to the ceiling, and, most seriously, we were in danger of losing our home.

And Then God . . .

It was September 1982. We'd just lost the business. I was paralyzed by fear and pain like I'd never known. I was fresh out of ideas. When I'd reached the end of myself and run out of schemes and solutions, God was able to get my attention.

It's not that I wasn't a Christian. I'd grown up in church, graduated from a Christian college, married a committed Christian, and was very active in church. The problem is I'd never allowed God to invade my life. I kept Him compartmentalized. My Christianity was convenient on Sundays or when missionaries visited. But when it came to my day-to-day life I had it figured out. I found security and dignity in the color and quantity of my credit cards and in my ability to borrow money. Now my house of cards was collapsing around me.

It was as if God turned on the floodlights of heaven, and for the first time I was able to acknowledge what I'd done. I saw what a horrible mess I'd made and what I'd done to my husband, my family, and myself.

Completely broken, I confessed that the manipulation, the scheming, deceit, and lying were sin. I begged for God's forgiveness (which of course was mine for the asking). I pleaded with God to let me keep my husband, my kids, and our home. I promised God on that day that I would do anything and everything necessary to pay back all the debt, to change my ways, and to find my security only in Him. Of course God forgave me the instant I sought forgiveness. All the debts were not mysteriously repaid or lost forever from the records of all the companies and individuals to whom we owed money. And my pain did not immediately disappear. But God forgave me.

I spent the next twelve years working hard and learning everything I could about myself. God marvelously provided a job for me—a real estate position in which I was able to earn both a regular salary as well as commissions. We learned how to cut expenses and live without incurring new debt. There were occasions when we were slow learners, and we didn't do everything perfectly. But the point is this: As I was willing to change, God made those changes possible.

The ways that God provided and taught me are probably another book in themselves. But let me make this point absolutely clear: I allowed terrible habits to guide my life—actions I practiced habitually until they became almost automatic. Those habits when practiced over a long period of time had an accumulative devastating effect.

Time to Pay Up

During the thirteen years since then, we've paid back the entire $100,000 in unsecured debts plus all the interest and associated fees. I've come face to face with my compulsive overspending problem and am learning one day at a time how to deal with that and depend on God to meet our needs instead of looking to credit as the solution.

As we've obeyed God's financial principles of giving, saving, and not spending more than we have, He's blessed us in ways you could never imagine. The irony is that now I have the wonderful privilege of helping people all over the country apply these same principles to their lives, get out of debt, and learn how to joyfully live beneath their means. It is possible to become responsible in areas where irresponsibility is the order of the day.

I'm Still Me

I have not had a personality transplant. I will always have compulsive tendencies. By God's grace, however, I'm learning how to control my compulsive nature, adopt good financial habits, and make up for lost time. After all, during the last twenty-five years, the years when we should have been preparing for the future by saving and investing, we were doing just the opposite. Considering the alternatives, we were thankful to return to point zero.

Wonderful things have happened since that day in 1982 when I hit bottom. I've learned to allow the Lord to invade my life, not to just visit on Sundays. I've learned the necessity of obedience to God's Word and the joy and peace of mind that comes from a daily relationship with Jesus Christ, the One who, after all, knows me best and loves me most.

PART TWO

Roles, Myths, and Reformation

TWO

Where Is It Written "Women Don't Do Money"?

First you change your attitude, then you change your life.

UNKNOWN

Lucy Ricardo taught me that being dumber than dirt is kind of cute. Her neighbor Ethel was a little smarter than Lucy but only occasionally managed to overcome Lucy's dumbness. And Gracie Allen (remember her?). Well, she was dumber than Lucy and Ethel put together.

Those girls could certainly spend the money, couldn't they? Thank goodness for Ricky, Fred, and George. Where would those women have been without the men to take care of them, protect them from themselves, and pay all the bills? Those television husbands always managed to clean up their wives' messes. It didn't matter to what degree Lucy's own stupidity overwhelmed her; Ricky always had the solution and just in the nick of time.

The women never had to think about money, and they never cared much about where it came from so long as it kept coming. I guess the men worked—that part of the plot was always a little foggy for me. Ricky left every morning for rehearsal; Fred hung out and collected rent. And George Burns? I haven't a clue what he did for a living. I don't think Gracie did either.

Those women didn't participate in the family finances, and that was the way we thought it was supposed to be. They spent their days poking into everyone's business and were hilariously consumed with how much trouble they could stir up.

The men were the protectors, the "bailer outers" and problem solvers. Of course, they handled all the finances. That was my favorite part. It was so romantic to be a bit helpless and silly. The secret was having a smart husband with unlimited sources of money who would always take care of everything.

Waiting for Prince Charming

As a little girl, I got the message that being protected and loved meant never having to know about money. I didn't get that message because I watched too much television—we didn't even have one. I learned it from real life. In my world, women took care of the relationships and men took care of the money. Women were the emotional caretakers, men the wage earners.

I learned that men go to work, women shop and spend, and no one ever talks about it. My mother didn't handle any money. She had what she called "pin money," but it was not considered essential to her financial well-being or that of our family. I learned that a good husband was measured by his ability to be a "good provider," which meant he earned the money, paid the bills, and made all the financial decisions.

I didn't learn appropriate and useful money skills because handling money was the exclusive territory of men. By default I learned that "women don't do money."

No wonder I breathed one big sigh of relief as I walked down the aisle. Not only was I marrying a terrific guy, I would no longer have to worry about "man stuff," like car trouble and money, because I'd found my provider, my caretaker, my man. I'd take care of the woman things and he'd do the man ones. We never actually talked about it. Some things didn't require discussion.

I guess you know where this kind of flawed thinking got me. Let's put it this way: I didn't find marriage to be one lively episode of "I Love Lucy." My shenanigans with money weren't solved in thirty-minute segments. I wasn't bailed out and given a fresh start every day as credits rolled by and the theme music played.

Distinctly Different

I am not a feminist,[1] "women's libber," or "N.O.W.[2] gal." However, I do believe men and women are equal, and distinct creations. Praise God! I don't want to be like a man. I love being a woman. I have God-given characteristics as a woman that I acknowledge and embrace.

As women, we want happiness, we want to feel significant, and we want to receive respect and honor from men. We want to feel that we have a genuine purpose in life. We want to receive joy and satisfaction in our work whether that work is in the home, outside the home, or both. We want to feel secure, and we also want to feel valuable for our intelligence and management abilities.

I don't find any place in Scripture where women are relieved of the responsibility to be wise money managers. I don't know any verse that says men are to handle the

1. One who advocates a gender-free society.
2. National Organization of Women, a radical organization of feminists.

money. Yet, there is a pervasive attitude, especially among Christians, that as head of the home, the man must make financial decisions and handle the money. Personally, I believe some men use control of family finances as a way of keeping their wives dependent and subordinate.

Please don't misunderstand me. I can't think of a more noble calling than to be a wife and mother. I'm not suggesting for a moment that every woman must leave the home and join the working world. Nor am I suggesting that every woman must marry in order to be fulfilled and live a meaningful life. And I'm not saying that women should control the family purse. What I *am* saying is this: *Every woman regardless of her marital status, age, strengths, or weaknesses needs to know how to manage money confidently and effectively.*

God requires all people, men and women alike, to be good stewards, to work hard, to make wise decisions, to give back to Him, and to save for the future. I believe that the financial principles found in the Bible apply to both genders. Financial responsibility is for all of us.

Not Her Again!

I would love to meet the woman described in Proverbs 31. I didn't always feel so kindly toward her, however. There was a time, I must admit, I dreaded Mother's Day, knowing that before I got out of the church service I'd surely find myself compared to the Proverbs 31 woman in some way or another. Clearly, everything about her pointed out how miserably I was failing in the area of resource management, and rubbing her perfection in my face only made it worse.

As I've changed, however, I've changed my mind about her too. She's become a role model to me—an example of a financially confident woman. I'm not sure I'll ever equal her amazing abilities, but she certainly sets an example worth emulating.

A truly good wife is the most precious treasure
  a man can find!
Her husband depends on her,
  and she never lets him down.
She is good to him every day of her life,
  and with her own hands she gladly makes clothes.
She is like a sailing ship
  that brings food from across the sea.
She gets up before daylight to prepare food
  for her family and for her servants.
She knows how to buy land
and how to plant a vineyard,
  and she always works hard.
She knows when to buy or sell,
  and she stays busy until late at night.
She spins her own cloth,
  and she helps the poor and the needy.
Her family has warm clothing,
  and so she doesn't worry when it snows.
She does her own sewing,
  and everything she wears is beautiful.
Her husband is a well-known and respected leader
  in the city.
She makes clothes to sell to the shop owners.
She is strong and graceful,
  as well as cheerful about the future.
Her words are sensible,
  and her advice is thoughtful.
She takes good care of her family and is never lazy.
Her children praise her,
  and with great pride her husband says,
"There are many good women, but you are the best!"
Charm can be deceiving and beauty fades away,
but a woman who honors the LORD
  deserves to be praised.
Show her respect—
  praise her in public for what she has done.

PROVERBS 31:10–31

A Model Worth Emulating

Tell me, do you see a woman here who doesn't "do money"? Not a chance. She is resourceful, entrepreneurial, and a financial wizard. Did you notice how she buys land, plants a vineyard, and then knows when to sell? I'd love to walk down Wall Street with her. She's not sitting on the sidelines of the family financial decision-making because she thinks "women don't do money."

She doesn't mortgage her husband's future by getting into all kinds of debt that will keep them in bondage for many years to come. She doesn't think that it's her job to spend and his job to provide. And she's cheerful about the future. Let me tell you, if she had $100,000 in unsecured debt breathing down her neck with a drawer full of bills she's afraid her husband might find, cheerful would not be one of the ways her children described her.

Not only does she make her own clothes, she spins the yarn and weaves the cloth. And get this: She's developed her own line of beautiful fashions, which she sells to local boutiques. Her husband and kids are proud of her, which doesn't surprise me a bit.

This is one financially confident woman. There is absolutely no question in my mind that God honors this kind of pursuit and has given her profile to us as an example, a standard, an ideal.

A Peek inside the Mailbag

I get a lot of mail (and when I say a lot I mean file drawers full) from men and women, old and young, from every state in the U.S. and many foreign countries. These people are, for the most part, readers of *Cheapskate Monthly*, a subscription newsletter I write and publish (shameless plug).

Many of these letters start out: "*Dear Mary, What I'm about to tell you I've never told another soul. . . .*" I'd estimate that about 85 percent of the letters I receive are from women, and of that number at least 50 percent are from women in pain who tell me of their frustration and struggles with money. I've learned so much about myself and others through this unique form of education. Take a peek into my letter files:

"I'm so discouraged. No matter how hard I try, there's never enough money. I just don't know what to do."

"I've tried to save, but every time I put some money away, something comes up. Right now I have $1,100 in bills I can't pay. The creditors are calling and I'm terrified."

"I'm a housewife with three girls. We live paycheck to paycheck. My husband refuses to admit just how bad things really are. I have no idea where his paycheck goes. If only I knew someone to lend us some money."

"I feel as if I am sinking in an abyss of financial ignorance."

"My heart is so heavy. . . . I hate myself when I fail over and over. I was doing so good at not using plastic but have fallen off the wagon again. We are at least $1,000 short every month and I am dying inside."

"We're always in some crisis about money, but my husband just ignores it. I just don't know where the money goes."

"He is a good provider most of the time, but during the slow months it's really terrible. I worry so much about money I'm making myself sick."

"I've always wanted to buy a home, but I think that will never happen. My husband left me with the kids and all the bills."

"When he died, I was shocked to find out the condition of our finances. For forty-eight years I had no idea what was going on because he always handled the money."

"I'm so sick of always being broke and having to pretend that everything is okay."

"If I have it, I spend it. It's like I can't help myself. For me going shopping is like playing roulette, I just never know what's going to happen."

"Money is just too hard for me. I feel like such a failure."

"I only wish I had the ability to earn more money. Things are very tough and I just don't know how we'll make it."

"I hope you can help me. I'm all alone for the first time in twenty-eight years. I don't even know where to start."

"I thought the insurance money would be plenty. I realize now that I should have looked for someone to tell me how to invest it. Between lending it to the kids and fixing up the house, it's just about gone and I have no idea what I'll do when it is."

These women have reached a critical point. They need the skills and the knowledge to competently manage money, but they don't know what to do to take control. Their situations are controlling them, and that is a terrible place to be.

Maybe you, too, have felt some of the same painful, frustrating, discouraging, hopeless, and scary feelings like those you've just read. Perhaps you've secretly wondered, *What's the matter with me? I can't control my spending, and I feel anxious and frustrated about money. I have no one to take care of me, and I don't know what I'm doing. I'm afraid something terrible is going to happen* . . . and on and on.

Fiscal Reality

A woman who has never been exposed to the subject of money management is typically afraid of making financial decisions, doesn't feel capable, and doesn't feel she can trust herself to make these kinds of changes. She'd just as soon someone else make all the financial decisions for her.

You might believe that money is not an important concern because you have a husband to make it, handle it, and manage it. Perhaps you are a young woman still living at home, waiting for Prince Charming to show up on his white horse with a promise that you will never have to worry your pretty little head about a thing. Let me encourage you to look beyond today. Chances are great that sometime during your lifetime things will change. You will be required to skillfully manage money, and you might not have a great deal of warning.

There's also the distinct probability that if you are married, your husband would love for you to start participating as a partner in the area of finances. For those of you who have children, consider what a terrific parenting team you and your husband make. The same could happen in your financial life.

Greater numbers of women are becoming money conscious because women are managing more money than ever before. Judith Briles in her book *Money Sense*[3] cites some information that should make all of us sit up and take notice:

- According to the Internal Revenue Service 35 percent of all estates valued at more than $5 million are controlled by women.
- Women are the beneficiaries of most life insurance policies.
- The U.S. House of Representatives' Committee on Small Business reports that by the year 2000, 50 percent of all small businesses in this country will be female-owned.

3. Judith Briles, *Money Sense* (Chicago: Moody Press, 1995), 16–18.

However, a survey conducted by the Oppenheimer Management Corporation in 1992 reported that:

- ▼ Only 9 percent of women feel very confident in making investment decisions.
- ▼ Women between the ages of thirty-five and fifty-four were found to be the least knowledgeable about investing.
- ▼ Seventy-one percent admitted they did not know how to invest.
- ▼ Thirty-seven percent of those surveyed had never made an investment decision, and not surprisingly the same number reported they devote absolutely no time to savings and investments.

Additional surveys from the Oppenheimer group taken since 1992 disclosed the following:

- ▼ Fifty-two percent of the women surveyed said they feel financially unprepared for retirement.
- ▼ Eighty-two percent of these financially ignorant women believe that they will be solely responsible for their own financial well-being at some point in their lives.
- ▼ Women save only half of what men do, on average.

According to the United States Bureau of the Census:

- ▼ Forty-eight percent of women aged sixty-five and older are or will be widowed.
- ▼ Fifty percent of women who married within the last twenty years will divorce.
- ▼ Ten percent will remain single.

The message is quite sobering, isn't it? At some point in your life, there is a good chance you will be responsible for your own financial security. You may be required to not only manage the finances, but you might also become the principal wage earner. This is why it is so important for you not to abandon your own financial identity.

Whether you are currently using them or not, you need to keep up your skills and your education so that in the event of a major life change you will have the confidence necessary to deal with it.

While it is slowly closing, the wage gap still exists in this country. Women earn seventy-four cents for every dollar earned by men. That alone is a good argument for why women, above all, need to possess excellent financial planning and management skills.

Whether presently you are solely responsible for your financial well-being, share it with your partner, or want to be prepared for any eventuality, there's no time like the present to start learning how to become a financially confident woman. A wife who says, "My husband handles that sort of thing," is likely giving away a huge part of her life.

The traditional relationship where the wife is not involved with the family finances (being given $100 a week for groceries and household expenses doesn't count as being involved in the family finances) is not only shortsighted; it is just plain stupid. The other extreme, where the husband opts out of all financial matters leaving all the bills and financial planning to his modern wife, is no better.

Typically one of the two partners in a marriage is more naturally gifted with numbers. Terrific! Then that person should keep the records but not make all the decisions.

Becoming more knowledgeable about money means more than just paying the bills or balancing the checkbook. It means understanding money and its role in our lives.

In my home I am the one who's not good with numbers, so Harold balances the checkbook. It's not that I don't know how or couldn't do it if he wasn't available. And he's terrible in the kitchen, so I do the cooking. It has nothing to do with gender, but talent. When it comes to major financial decisions and the monthly bills, we review everything together and the decision making is a joint effort.

The Nurturing Female

Men and women bring different things to a marriage. Being a woman, I know that I have God-given strengths by virtue of my female genes. I'm a nurturer. I'm more sensitive to detail and able to keep track of where things are and where they're supposed to be. I love to watch things grow. Knowing everyone is safe and tucked in at night somehow gives me a feeling of well-being and security. I think those are characteristics God placed inside of me, and guess what? Those parts of my personality make me the best one to look after our investments. They need to be nurtured, allowed to grow in the safest place possible so they are all cozy and warm. Harold and I are a team; and since we've learned to be team players in this area of personal finance, our relationship has grown tremendously, as has our financial picture.

Stop for a moment and think about how smart, clever, capable, and responsible you are in so many other areas of your life. Perhaps you single-handedly run a household, possess excellent skills as scheduler, cleaner, chauffeur, chef, dietitian, nutritionist, tutor, athletic coordinator, laundress, seamstress, landscape artist, florist, purchasing agent, and nurse. Perhaps you are very successful in your career and have gained the respect of your peers in the professional world. There is absolutely no reason you cannot add competent money manager and financial planner to your list of abilities and skills.

Money management needs to become as important in your life as all the other skills you've learned. A financially confident woman is a woman who has the knowledge, ability, and desire to behave in a financially responsible manner. The designation is available to anyone.

"God is good. So I beg you to offer your bodies to him as a living sacrifice, pure and pleasing. That's the most sensible way to serve God. Don't be like the people of this world, but let God change the way you think. Then you will know how to do everything that is good and pleasing to him" (Rom. 12:1–2).

Money Do's and Don'ts for Women

Do	Don't
Be a giver.	Be a taker.
Save a portion of every paycheck and other money at the time it flows into your life.	Wait to see what's left at the end of the month.
See yourself as an equal contributor to the welfare and well-being of your family.	Consider yourself a second-class partner if you don't happen to earn a separate paycheck.
Nurture your financial identity.	Depend on your partner or another person to make your financial decisions.
Develop and maintain skills so that you are capable of earning a living.	Let your education go to waste by allowing your job skills to become obsolete.
Learn everything you possibly can about all areas of personal financial planning.	Shirk your responsibility to be an educated and equal partner in family financial decisions
Communicate openly about all areas of personal financial planning.	Assume anything.
Plan ahead for emergencies.	Fool yourself by thinking challenges of a financial nature will never come upon you and your family.
Take pride in your position as manager or co-manager of the most important organization on the face of the earth—your family.	Ever put yourself down.
Consider debt something to be avoided if at all possible. It really is a four-letter word.	Look upon your credit limit as part of your income or an entitlement to have what you cannot afford with your regular income.
Order copies of your credit reports at least annually.	Assume the credit reporting agencies never make a mistake.

THREE

Responsible Is Not Another Word for Dull and Boring

When we were children,
we thought and reasoned as children do.
But when we grew up, we quit our childish ways.

1 CORINTHIANS 13:11

At first glance the ad for a part-time college library assistant seemed like the perfect job for me. Since I was transportationally challenged, working on campus would have its advantages.

My interview was not as idyllic, however. Miss Holt could have been cast as the stereotypically stern, joyless librarian. She had the part down pat. She also had great intuition. Prior to hiring me as her assistant she gave me quite a little lecture on responsibility.

It didn't take long for me to develop a healthy fear of the woman and an equally healthy determination that I wouldn't let her consecration to responsibility rub off on me. Like a uniform, I slipped into my responsible self during work hours and shed it as quickly as possible when my time was up.

Why is it that the whole idea of being responsible sounds so matronly, so boring, so downright dull? *Responsible* was what divided the dull personalities from those who had a life. In my world, *responsible* was what kept the less-than-fun group hopelessly dormitory bound. The risk takers were anything but responsible. I guess you might say *irresponsible* was where the action was. It didn't take me long to decide where I wanted to align myself. I looked at it this way: Responsibility tied people down, so irresponsibility should free them up. Thus, my experiences with throwing caution to the wind and living for the moment began.

With that background I find it quite amazing that this is a book about responsible living. God's willingness to redeem even the most unlikely people is something that continues to amaze me. Make no mistake, however, this is *not* a book on how to become matronly, boring, and dull. This is a book about financial responsibility. It is not a book about budgets. If you ask me, there are already too many books on budgets. This is a book about the miracles that can happen when irresponsible financial habits are forever replaced with responsible ones.

Since my younger days, I have learned that it is possible to be responsible *and* fun-loving. It is possible to be financially mature *and* contemporary. It is possible to be responsible *and* spontaneous. Responsibility simply means being accountable, and that is a good thing.

No matter what the terms *responsible* and *irresponsible* mean to you, I hope that for the next couple hundred pages you'll be able to set aside any preconceived notions, sit back, and enjoy. Maybe you'll learn something new. Then again, you might discover you're one of those to-be-envied sorts for whom financial responsibility comes naturally *and* you're a fun person too. If so, your habits are what the rest of us wish to emulate. We want to be like you.

The Basic Plan

My goal is that by the time you finish this book you will have the basic tools to

- ▼ assess your relationship with money,
- ▼ take control of irresponsible behaviors,
- ▼ replace them with behaviors that are responsible, and
- ▼ see that those positive financial behaviors become lifelong habits.

First, we're going to take a quick look at how our beliefs, attitudes, and values determine how we behave with money. Next, we'll tackle the whole idea of how repeated behaviors become habits whether they're positive behaviors or not. We'll see how we can choose to change behavior by going back to check out the beliefs that are responsible for inappropriate behavior. It's like finding the offending "bug" and fixing the system. We'll then identify the habits of financially responsible women and set out to purposely do the things they do until our bad habits are replaced with actions that are in accordance with God's word.

The Am-I-Financially-Irresponsible? Self-Diagnostic Test

Directions: Answer yes or no to the following statements.

1. I have nothing close to a reasonable knowledge of my income, fixed expenses, irregular expenses, and net worth.
2. I don't have the discipline to be good with money.
3. I am near, at, or over the limit on my credit cards.
4. I've bounced more than three checks in the past year.
5. I often use this month's income to cover last month's bills.

6. I can't imagine living without credit.
7. I've never been concerned about money because I have a spouse who takes care of it.
8. I worry about money quite a bit.
9. I hide the mail.
10. I don't have a formal savings program.
11. If I had more money I'd be just fine.
12. I have lied to my spouse or creditors about making payments.
13. I know I should give money to God but there's just not enough right now.
14. I've taken a cash advance on one credit card to make the payment on another card.

Scoring: If you answered no to every question, you are my heroine. You are a financially responsible person. If you answered yes to one or two questions, your tendencies lean toward responsible, but you should consider these areas to be red flags. Three to five yes answers are a definite sign that you're headed down the road to financial trouble. I pray you will see the need to turn around immediately. Yes on six or more? There's no doubt about it—we need each other. I recommend you not leave home until you finish this book.

FOUR

Time Out for a Values Inventory

You created me and put me together.
Make me wise enough to learn what you have commanded.
PSALM 119:73

What are your money beliefs? Do you even have a clue? Could you articulate them if it were really important to do so? Could you write them down? Enough questions already?

How you deal with money—your money behavior—is determined by what you think about money—your money beliefs. Your money behavior is an outward display of what you believe about money and its role in your life. For most, those beliefs are nebulous and buried somewhere in our subconscious minds.

BEHAVIORS

Behaviors are symptoms of our internal beliefs. Trying to manage symptoms while ignoring the underlying cause is a waste of time and energy. Haven't we learned that from all the diets and budgets we've tried? Sure, they might work for a day or a week, maybe longer, but in time diets and budgets fail because they just don't get down into the roots.

Beliefs

A *belief* is a feeling of certainty about what something means. It is a statement we make about ourselves or the world. Clearly, it is possible to have personal beliefs that are not based in truth. Dangerous perhaps, but indeed possible. Once a false belief is identified, it is possible to dump it and replace it with one that is true.

Attitudes

A group of beliefs regarding the same object or subject produces an *attitude.* Once an attitude is formed, behavior regarding that object becomes pretty much automatic. If my attitude toward dogs is one of fear, it's quite likely I had a bad experience with a dog somewhere along the line. So every time I encounter a dog, I experience fear—an automatic response based on a group of beliefs. Each of us has a belief system that is made up of many beliefs that in turn produce many attitudes.

Values

Values are specific types of beliefs that are so important and central to one's belief system they act as life guides. Values are central to a person's personality and are responsible for motivations and important decisions that have far-reaching implications.

Typically a person will have hundreds of thousands of beliefs, a thousand or so attitudes, and around a dozen values. When it comes to money, many of us live under false beliefs that greatly affect our lives.

Money Training

Your money beliefs are a mirror that reflects the money attitude and beliefs of one or both of your parents, and your money beliefs reflect the beliefs and attitudes of the segment of society you live in. All of these have taught you a lot about how you as a woman should behave with money, what you should and should not do, and what you can and cannot do.

Generally speaking, all money beliefs are a variation on one of two themes: Money is evil; money is good. Whether we worship money or hate it, when we hold it responsible for our happiness we give it power. Whether consciously or subconsciously, we choose the role money plays in our lives. So we, not our money or lack of it, are solely responsible for our attitudes, beliefs, actions, and happiness.

As a little girl, you were like a sponge. You soaked in beliefs. You watched and listened. Maybe you absorbed fear, perhaps adoration. You may have formed beliefs about being undeserving or incompetent. What you learned, starting with your first moment on earth, has contributed to your adult attitudes and beliefs about how to get what you want and need. All of these beliefs have determined what you feel you deserve, if you think you are smart enough to manage money, or if you believe you must forever depend on someone else to get what you need.

The beliefs and therefore the attitudes you have about money have a lot to do with why you always spend more money than you have, why you don't believe you will ever get ahead, why you feel so controlled by your finances, why you can't get enough money, or why you don't believe you deserve anything.

Not long ago I received a letter from a woman who told me of her struggle with letting go of false money beliefs. As the oldest child of missionaries, she spent her early childhood and teenage years in a foreign country. Somehow during those years she developed a false belief that those who serve God must endure poverty. After all, why else would her family be so poor while the carnal Christians "back home" in secular occupations lived in luxury? Her parents would often tell her that while they had little money and material possessions they were rich because they were serving the Lord.

Years passed and this woman became a mother and wife. She became one of those "carnal Christians." She felt guilty for having nice things, for making more money in a month than her family had for an entire year on the mission field. Once she was able to dig through all her emotions and get to the heart of the matter, she discovered her false beliefs regarding money were keeping her from enjoying all the blessings God had given to her.

Once you accept the fact that perhaps some of the things you believe about money might be defective or downright false, you will be able to begin the process of changing your money beliefs and thus your money behaviors. You will be able to let go of old beliefs that keep you stuck in either hating or worshiping money.

If you have been irresponsible or reckless with money, have allowed credit to control your life, have gotten into a tiny financial mess or one of behemoth proportions, or have failed to participate in the financial aspects of your home, it is not because there's something wrong with you. You are not fiscally defective! It's just that somewhere along the way you've picked up false beliefs about money and the role it plays in your life.

Taking Responsibility

We are responsible for our own beliefs, feelings, and attitudes. We have to look to ourselves when it comes to doing something about our problems with money or lack of understanding about it. Blaming money, or the lack of it, for our problems and behaviors is no different than blaming others or God for our misery. We choose the role money plays in our lives, and taking responsibility for that is the first step in making necessary changes. The first step in taking responsibility for our beliefs is finding out what they are.

Are you ready to examine your current beliefs and attitudes about money? Perhaps you're unsure what yours are. Frankly, I'd be a little surprised if you weren't. Following are common beliefs and attitudes about money. Perhaps you'll find some of each of the attitudes in your own life, perhaps none. Regardless, learning about others' beliefs may help you figure out what your own attitudes are. Once you know what they are, you'll be able to examine them, identify those that are based in truth, and let go of false, destructive beliefs and attitudes.

Destructive and Self-Defeating Money Attitudes

Money as an Object of Worship

If someone had accused me of worshiping money, I would have said, "No way. I'm a Christian and that's the last thing a Christian would ever do!" I've since learned that is also a false belief because many people worship money, Christians and nonbelievers alike.

Worship is the adoration, homage, or veneration given to a deity. It's that deep and reverent kind of love we're supposed to reserve for God. Changing the focus from God to money is a rather foolish thing to consider.

The act of worship, something our souls long for, has three elements:

1. A worshiper
2. Something to worship
3. The worshiper's willingness to be controlled by the thing or person worshiped.

If I choose money to be the thing I worship, for example, I voluntarily choose to place myself under the control of money. I give up control and allow money to have authority over my life. I become subservient to it.

Sounds pretty sick when we put it into words, doesn't it? The person who worships money is convinced that money, and enough of it, holds the key to a perfect life. She might also believe it is responsible for love, freedom, success, and joy.

I spent a great deal of my life worshiping money. Getting more and more of it became my central focus. I was in awe of what it was supposed to do in my life; and because my ego was insatiable, more money was never enough. I guaranteed myself a life of unhappiness because I was always waiting to be happy until I had enough money. I was obsessed with money. No wonder I was so miserable.

"The love of money causes all kinds of trouble. Some people want money so much that they have given up their faith and caused themselves a lot of pain" (1 Tim. 6:10). "Don't fall in love with money. Be satisfied with what you have. The Lord has promised that he will not leave us or desert us" (Heb. 13:5).

The message is clear: We must not worship anything or anyone other than God himself. Nothing and no one other than God should be allowed to sit on the throne of our lives. It is impossible to worship both God and money (see Luke 16:13). There's only room for one on that throne.

God says that we are not to worship any god except Him, that he is a jealous God who wants us to love and obey His laws (see Exod. 20:2–6). God's rules make a lot of sense. They aren't harsh or inconsiderate of our needs, and by following them the quality of our lives can be greatly improved. When God is not honored as God and we divert our worship to anything or anyone else, misery results. Take it from me, it is easy to allow money to become a god.

Money as a Mood Changer

Money can be as powerful a mood changer as the most potent tranquilizer—and as habit forming. Spending money whether we have it or not has become a socially acceptable practice, especially if we can justify the act because we've had a terrible week and deserve to buy a little something nice for ourselves. When it comes to needing to snap out of it or get over it, spending money often does the trick. Yet it is a poor tranquilizer because the satisfaction of the purchase wears off quickly, and then it takes a bigger fix the next time to achieve the same level of mood change.

I spoke with a friend one day who through tears described how she is compelled to buy something for herself every day. If she doesn't, she feels so badly she can't stand it. Buying something somehow provides an anesthetic effect for her bad feelings and gives her something to look forward to. She has been completely unable to give up this shopping ritual even though she has become buried in secret debt and has closets full of new merchandise for which she has absolutely no use.

There's real danger in using money to alter our moods because it is very easy to become addicted to the act. We are addictive beings. Some people medicate strong feelings with a drug of choice, others with a compulsive behavior. For many women, shopping is an effective way to deal with fears and feelings of insignificance and loneliness. They buy something pretty in the same way a mother hands over a pacifier to a fussy baby.

Money Measures Success

Do you relate poverty with evil and prosperity with good? Align poverty with stupidity and prosperity with intelligence? That's what all our childhood fairy tales taught, didn't they?

No wonder those who believe that wealth and success go hand in hand feel personal failure whenever they experience a lack of money. On the other hand, if they have a streak of "good luck," women who share this particular attitude about money then feel they have value because of this "success." If you believe that your value depends on how much money you have, your status and self-image fluctuates along with your bank balance.

This false money belief can be very tempting because of the emphasis society places on the marriage of success and money. It's a rare person who does not immediately define success by using the word *money.*

What is success anyway? Is it reached when one makes $200,000 a year or when a child's life is changed for eternity through the faithfulness of a Sunday School teacher? Is it winning an Academy Award or writing lyrics to a song that will touch the hearts of people for centuries to come? I don't know all the answers; but it seems to me that when we get really honest, true success is often far removed from dollar signs.

It is a freeing thing to separate the issue of money from your life's work. Once money is a nonissue, you will be free to concentrate on what really matters and what will last long after you're gone.

Money Buys Love and Approval

Do you feel driven to go on a spending spree, justifying it as benevolence? *It's for the grandchildren*, or *I'm buying for others.* Are you buying gifts or are you attempting to buy approval and love? Are you being generous or purchasing obligation? Why is it that you always have to take the largest gift to the party or crave the feeling of status you get when you pick up the tab at the restaurant?

The person who is driven to use money to gain affection, approval, and love doesn't feel she deserves approval and love for being just who she is. She is driven to sweeten the pot with money and things. Parents with this false money belief often overindulge their children with everything under the sun with the underlying goal of earning their children's love and approval.

Money Is Evil, Poverty Is Righteous

There is a money belief that goes like this: Money is evil, and those who have it are greedy, dishonest, sinister, and generally corrupt. If you have this belief, to be good you must be poor. Poverty is equated with goodness. There is an underlying fear that opening one's life to money is a clear invitation for evil to come in and take over. Hate and fear of money become the unspoken rationales for losing, mishandling, and being unable to handle money. I've known people who even refuse to accept it. They seem to possess an internal terror of losing their goodness to money.

Perhaps you grew up in a family with very low financial means. Your parents, in dealing with the situation, taught you the foolishness of money and the vanity that accompanies it—telling you that there are more important things in life than money. Money was a vice. Of course these things are true in some ways, but the message you received was that if you are to be a woman of virtue you need to avoid money lest it be allowed to corrupt your life.

Perhaps you didn't learn that money is the result of a job well-done and that money can be used in a remarkable way to demonstrate your commitment to God's principles. There are women who have become addicted to poverty and have a very difficult time giving up the false belief that money is evil as are those who have it.

Those who hold this money belief equate their poverty with martyrdom and a high level of virtue. The woman with this belief feels more righteous than the "money-grubbing" individuals around her who are obsessed with materialism. Because of this belief, she is likely a compulsive underearner hesitant to accept payment for work she does. Her volunteerism is usually excessive, and she feels that her eternal rewards negate the necessity of fair payment here on earth. What money she does have or manages she hoards, compulsively stashing and investing and then "righteously" living on a ridiculously low, poverty-level income.

Money Is Limited

Another destructive belief goes something like this: The money I have is all I'll ever have; when it's gone, that's all there is.

As a kid I remember feeling this way about colognes and other precious commodities. Because I feared that when these products were gone there would be no more, I never used them. I only looked at them. I still wonder whatever happened to those little navy blue bottles of Evening in Paris.

This belief causes paralyzing fear of inflation, interest rates, cost of living, and the future. The most terrible thing about this belief is that it's self-fulfilling. Because we fear there will be no more money, we make sure that's exactly what happens. It's a lot like thinking, *I just know I can't do it*—and sure enough, you can't.

Women who believe money is scarce are often debilitated by the possibility of making mistakes. Because there's no room for error, there's no ability to take risks.

Healthy Money Beliefs and Attitudes

You might be amazed to know that the Bible has over one thousand references to the subject of money. It's a money reference guide. God's Word, the source of all truth, is the place to find guidance for establishing our beliefs and attitudes.

Money Is a Tool

Money is a handy convenience. Without it we'd have to carry around chickens and pigs to trade for goods and services that we need. We exchange money for our skills and abilities, so, in a way, it is a tangible representation of our life's energy. Money is a tool that God gives to us—all of us, men and women alike—because He is the giver of skills and abilities.

Money Is Powerless

Money has no power of its own, in the same way your sewing machine or electric mixer have no inherent ability. (I'd be very interested in a lawn mower or vacuum cleaner that had the ability to self-operate, wouldn't you?) The truth is that no matter how fancy, how turbocharged, how modern or technically capable, any tool left in the closet or used contrary to the purpose for which it was intended is not going to produce the best results; and in some cases, the results can be negative. Take the woman who intended to wax her car and picked up the power sander instead of the power buffer. They looked alike.

Money Is a Neutral Commodity

It's what we do with a tool that counts. The way we manage money is a direct reflection of our commitment to obey God and serve others. God honors right attitudes, and when a godly belief system and a set of life values are reflected through our finances, God is glorified. He blesses those whom He can trust.

We are not to worry about from where money will come. Employers (or pensions, bonuses, real estate income, support, unemployment checks, or any other entity) are not the source of our income. They are simply the conduits through which God delivers it. God is the source because He is the one who has given us the skills and abilities to work. Jobs may come and go, stock markets may crash, real estate values may fall off the face of the earth, but the Source is the same yesterday, today, and forever. Our job is to be faithful, diligent, and trustworthy stewards.

Listen to the words of Jesus:

> "I tell you not to worry about your life. Don't worry about having something to eat, drink, or wear. Isn't life more than food or clothing? Look at the birds in the sky! They don't plant or harvest. They don't even store grain in barns. Yet your Father in heaven takes care of them. Aren't you worth more than birds? . . . Why do you have such little faith?
>
> "Don't worry and ask yourselves, 'Will we have anything to eat? Will we have anything to drink? Will we have any clothes to wear?' Only people who don't know God are always worrying about such things. Your Father in heaven knows that you need all of these. But more than anything else, put God's work first and do what he wants. Then all the other things will be yours as well."
>
> MATTHEW 6:25–33

The proper management of money is quite simple:

1. Give some away.
2. Keep some.
3. It is better not to borrow; but if you cannot avoid it, repay the debt quickly.
4. Do not spend money that doesn't belong to you.
5. Do not become preoccupied with money.
6. Don't fall in love with money!

Money is to be a nonemotional subject. We are not to love money or hate it, be fearful of not having enough or worried about having too much. We are to be comfortable with money, not anxious about it or careless with it. We are not to hoard it, nor are we to throw it away. That kind of financial balance is called solvency. Solvency occurs when money takes its proper place in our lives as a tool with which to serve the Lord, not as a filler of empty souls.

Happiness and Contentment

Each of us has a body, an ego, and a spirit. Our egos are in search of happiness; our souls long for contentment.

Your ego is not a bad thing. It's that part of you that includes your personality—your thinking, feeling, and acting self. Your ego is responsible for your style and personal tastes. Your ego produces emotions and desires—and I mean all kinds of desires, from little, so-so ones to those that scream out to be satisfied. Some desires are for needs, others for wants.

Face it. Satisfying a desire produces happiness, and it usually takes money to fulfill desires. Anyone who says money can't buy happiness has never bought new carpeting or a new car, or seen the look on a child's face on Christmas morning. The frustrating thing is that this kind of happiness is temporary. It always wears off.

Think back to a time when you longed for something. I mean really longed and yearned. You were nearly obsessed by your desire and could think of little else. Maybe it was your first car or a certain article of clothing or a new piece of furniture. When you finally got it you were happy beyond belief. But the happiness wore off, didn't it? That's because desires once satisfied do not stay satisfied. Gratification received from fulfilled desires is, at best, temporary. That's how our minds and emotions work.

Your soul, your spiritual nature seeks contentment—satisfaction with what you have, whatever your situation might be. Contentment is a learned behavior, an acquired skill. It doesn't just happen when you fall into the right set of circumstances. Contentment cannot be purchased and; that's the best news because it means contentment is available to everyone, no matter what their financial situation might be.

I believe that this longing for contentment within every person was placed there by God Himself. Further, I also believe He made that desire so unique that only a personal relationship with Him through His Son, Jesus Christ, can bring lasting satisfaction and the contentment our souls long for.

Once you understand that fulfilling the desires of ego produces temporary satisfaction and fulfilling the desires of your spirit brings lasting satisfaction, you can stop hoping to find lasting contentment in a new sofa, or joy and peace in new carpeting. Sure, your new sofa and carpeting will likely bring you happiness for some period of time. And that's wonderful. But you will quit looking to material things to produce the contentment your spirit seeks. You will instinctively know the difference between momentary pleasure and deep-seated contentment. What a change that will make in your life.

Contentment has a way of quieting insatiable desires. Contentment is the best antidote for an overly needy ego.

How to Change Beliefs and Behaviors

I discovered a secret, and I'm going to share it with you. If you want to change your money behavior, don't start with the behavior itself. I know that's what you've always tried to do in the past. Like another diet or another budget, however, attempting to manipulate the symptoms without taking notice of the belief behind the behavior will only result in failure. The behavior might change temporarily, but not permanently. You must trace the behavior back to the beliefs that are responsible for that action.

One of the best ways to get in touch with feelings and beliefs is to write. I think you'll find journaling to be very helpful in identifying your money beliefs. The written word has a wonderful way of giving substance and form to nebulous thoughts. You can identify which, if any, of your beliefs are false; and you can write about the healthy beliefs, attitudes, and values you want to bring into your life. With time and commitment to this project you will have developed powerful information and insight and you'll be ready to form new and healthy lifelong habits.

One word of caution: The more central a belief, the more resistant it is to change; and the more impact such change will have on the overall belief system. If one of your central beliefs changes, expect rather profound changes in how you think about many things.

Learning to view ourselves as deserving of every good and perfect gift from our heavenly Father doesn't mean indulging in every selfish desire we might have. Living abundantly means resting in the calm assurance that God, the Creator of the universe, loves you and me. He owns everything there is and knows our needs and the desires of our hearts. Living abundantly frees us to neither hate nor love money, but to see it as a neutral nonissue. Only when money is not the central focus of our lives can we stand back and see it as it truly is, and let it take its rightful place in our lives.

> "'I will bless you with a future filled with hope—
> a future of success, not of suffering.'"
>
> JEREMIAH 29:11

FIVE

Re-forming Your Habits

We are what we repeatedly do.
Excellence, then, is not an act, but a habit.

ARISTOTLE

Have you ever noticed how bad habits seem to come from nowhere, sneak in when you're not paying attention, and make themselves right at home? Mine remind me of weeds that push their way into a beautiful garden and arrogantly use their strength and amazing resistance to gain the upper hand. My good habits, on the otherhand, are more like delicate roses that require coaxing, cultivation, nurturing, and undaunted encouragement to build strong roots and grow into something of beauty. If only my good habits were as prolific as my bad ones.

Habits are those consistent, almost unconscious responses and behaviors that determine our effectiveness or ineffectiveness. A habit is a powerful force with the unique ability to be a best friend or a worst enemy. Our habits—how we behave day to day—are the outward and constant expressions of our character. What we do habitually reflects who we are.

Some of us act as though our habits were issued at birth and, good or bad, are as predetermined as our blood type and about as likely to ever change. Nothing could be further from the truth. It is possible to learn good habits and unlearn bad ones no matter how ingrained or deep seated they may be.

Habits are acts or practices we so frequently repeat that they become almost automatic. Almost automatic means that I, the owner and manager of my habits and behaviors, have not given up control to them like some mindless robot. I use them as a tool or a convenience not unlike an automatic transmission, automatic bread-making machine, or automatic dishwasher.

I got into major financial trouble because I habitually repeated behaviors involving money, credit, and debt that produced enjoyable feelings and brought instant gratification. These activities were pleasurable because they blocked pain, masked fear, and filled desire. At first glance that sounds like a pretty good method for coping, doesn't it? Don't kid yourself. Masking pain, anger, and fear by covering them with temporarily pleasurable feelings does nothing but make the masked emotions that much worse when the short-lived, pleasurable feelings wear off. And if that good feeling has had anything to do with credit cards and wild spending, a whole lot of guilt and anxiety get mixed in.

The Power of a Habit

Habits can be learned and unlearned; bad habits broken and good ones established. Just think of the wonderful new behaviors we can unleash once we understand the power of a habit.

The secret to becoming a financially confident woman is this:

1. Investigate how financially confident women behave.
2. Eliminate habits based on false money beliefs.
3. Imitate and practice those positive and beneficial behaviors so frequently they become almost automatic.

Consciously identify those financial habits you desire to be almost-automatic responses in your life and then choose to repeat them frequently until they become almost automatic. That's the way to acquire good financial habits—or any kind of habit, for that matter.

Practically speaking, if you repeat a behavior twenty-one times in a row it will become a habit. Repeat it for an additional twenty-one consecutive times and you have the likelihood of a lifelong behavior. That means three weeks to establish a new habit if it is repeated on a daily basis, and another three weeks to make sure you've got it.

It Can't Be That Easy!

It does sound simple doesn't it? If it were easy, we would've dumped our bad habits years ago, right? Well, perhaps. I'm the first to admit that just because I possess personal habits that happen to be bad and self-destructive doesn't mean I'm necessarily ready to get rid of them—easy or not. That's where the heartfelt desire to do the right thing comes in.

It's not like we haven't spent the better part of our lives making resolutions, promising ourselves to give this up, or start doing that. Only a fool would opt to hang onto bad habits if replacing them with good ones were easy. It's not always easy. Neither is most anything else that results in lasting value and lifelong positive change. Yet, it's surely worth the effort.

There was a time I secretly feared I had some kind of serious disorder, or at the very least, I was hopelessly addicted to spending money. It did seem rather appealing to blame something or someone for my bizarre behavior. Being a victim, after all, is quite fashionable these days and did offer an alternative. However, I finally came to this startling conclusion about myself: I behave the way I do because of my habits.

Thankfully there is a practical way to reprogram our almost-automatic negative or destructive responses. In the following chapters you're going to read about nine specific habits that are the habits of a financially confident woman. These habits are very personal to me because I previously possessed none of them. These are the behaviors that have completely changed my life. Here's how I learned the secret of reprogramming my habits.

Dumping Donuts

I've told you just about everything else about myself, so here goes with the donuts. I love 'em. I've always loved donuts. Donuts are fairly cheap, very available, and quite fattening. It's the fattening part that really made me want to break my daily habit. I should have been equally driven by the fact that I was spending a fortune at around a dollar a day. (Have you any idea what three hundred dollars a year will do when exposed to compounding interest?) But why do I *really* love donuts? They taste great. There's nothing like a high-fat, sugary donut to fill a nasty craving.

I heard James Dobson mention this twenty-one-day theory on his radio program. It sounded pretty easy, and of course I was willing to try anything my favorite psychologist recommended. My donut habit seemed like it would make an excellent proving ground. I decided that for twenty-one days straight I would not eat a donut. Bingo, I'd be forever delivered from a terrible habit.

It wasn't quite that easy. The third day was the worst. That's when it dawned on me I was giving up my beloved donuts forever—not for just three weeks. I was obsessed and could think of nothing else but donuts. If my memory serves correctly, I lasted about five days and picked right up on that donut habit like I hadn't missed a beat.

I didn't blame Dr. Dobson. It certainly wasn't his fault I was weak and undisciplined. I was just thankful I hadn't told him or anyone else of my little experiment in trying to break a bad habit. I sure wouldn't want to fail out there where anyone could see me.

Quite a few years later I recalled the twenty-one-day formula and decided I would use it to *establish* a new habit rather than break an old one. I thought this tactic would have a greater potential success rate since it's easier to do something than not do something.

My second attempt to experience the miracle of twenty-one involved my need to wear my car's seat belt. I know, this is something I should just do automatically. It's not that I would consciously choose not to put it on; it's just that I wouldn't think about it and my car didn't have an annoying warning buzzer or light. This time I was successful! After about a dozen days I noticed that my hand just went for the belt along with the chain of other movements required to get a car into motion.

After about three weeks, wearing my seat belt became a fairly automatic response; and after six weeks, I'd really made progress. It just didn't feel right to not wear it. I successfully created a new habit that continued for some time. Until we changed cars. The new seat belt didn't feel the same. The start-up routine was different. Before I knew it I repeated the not-belting act enough times (probably twenty-one) that the habit was unlearned. It was sometime later that I realized what had happened and I had to go through the relearning process all over again.

There are similar activities in your life that are so often repeated they've become nearly automatic. Take brushing your teeth for example. You do it so frequently and have for so many years that it is almost as automatic as breathing. And if we could capture this lovely behavior on video, I'm willing to bet you do it in the exact same way every time. You pick up the brush with the same hand, open the toothpaste in precisely the same manner, start at the same place, and finish exactly the way you've done it for at least 365 times a year since those pearly whites poked their way into your tiny mouth. It's a habit.

Make a private list of your good habits. Not only will it be fun; seeing them on paper will be affirming. Next, make a list of the habits you would like to establish. Don't go nuts with pages and pages of entries because that will only discourage you. It's hard to imagine I could live long enough to establish all the habits I could write down. Think of those behaviors that are most important to you right now. Perhaps it's your checking account statement. If you are not in the habit of balancing that sucker every month, this would be a good time to make a personal commitment to break the habit of ignoring the monthly statement. Don't worry if you don't know how to reconcile the bank statement with your checkbook register. That's coming a few chapters from now.

In the case of a monthly activity, the theory says it will take twenty-one consecutive repetitions to establish the habit. But that's twenty-one months, you shriek. So? It's a worthy habit to get into, and I know you can do it.

Becoming accountable to another person is a powerful way to make personal change. I don't mean that you need to shout it from the rooftops or publish it in the paper. Find someone whom you can trust to support you and stand by you in your desire to change. Your friend or buddy is not going to participate in changing you. That will never work. Yet, for some reason, the simple act of telling another person brings your personal commitment to a more conscious level. It becomes more important. Tell that person you're setting out to consciously break a bad behavior by not doing it repeatedly until the practice is no longer almost automatic. Or tell your friend that you want to pick up a new behavior, and you will be repeating it until it becomes almost automatic.

You might want to think about enlisting the help of a child in your quest to break a bad habit or develop a good habit. Let me assure you if you tell a young child that you want help in refraining from donuts you'll not only create for yourself a great reminder, you'll think long and hard before trying to sneak a donut when the little fellow's not looking.

Plot the Calendar

As you think of breaking a bad habit or establishing a good one, twenty-one days, twenty-one weeks, or twenty-one months might seem like an insurmountable task. But remember your last birthday? And when is your next? Time really flies, doesn't it? Those twenty-one weeks or months (or years!) will go quickly. They're going to go just as quickly if you begin establishing new behaviors or not. So you've nothing to lose but a bad habit and everything to gain including a good one.

A calendar is a handy tool to help you visualize the birth of a habit. Mark on the calendar the starting date, the twenty-one points between, and the ending date. As you begin moving through the twenty-one repetitions, mark them off in an act of celebration as you move toward success.

Check Your Focus

I want you to know that I will never suggest you do something that I'm not willing to do myself. I know that some of the behaviors having to do with money are going to be great challenges for many, and I am facing a great challenge in the area of establishing habits even as I write.

Changing behaviors starts with changing beliefs. The next step is to consciously change your focus. Whatever you focus on is what you move toward. In the matter of finances, you must consciously decide to begin focusing on positive money behaviors. The woman who successfully loses weight and goes on to become a weight-loss lecturer or counselor is a perfect example of how to stay focused.

When I began publishing my newsletter, *Cheapskate Monthly* (another shameless plug), I had no idea the fringe benefits I would receive from focusing on personal finance. I began the newsletter, quite frankly, in order to raise enough additional income to finish paying off our debts. I'd been fairly successful in changing destructive money behaviors, knew what techniques for getting out of debt and cutting expense had worked for us, and wanted to share this information with others.

As you can well imagine, my daily focus changed almost overnight. In starting my new business my focus zeroed in on one topic: personal-finance management. So that I could produce the best publication possible, my energy was channeled into research and communication.

Four years later I realize that my personal progress has been significant because I've been constantly focused. Publishing *Cheapskate Monthly* has done more for me than for any of its readers, I'm sure.

Had I focused on other areas and only delved into financial matters on an occasional basis, I'm quite certain we would not have made the financial progress we have. We're reaching goals we hadn't even considered setting.

Work in Process

I'm presently in the process of trying to establish physical fitness as a lifelong behavior. It's been nearly two years since I made a decision to do something about my terrible physical condition. Obviously, some habits take longer than others to establish!

I'm in excellent health. In fact, I have the world's most efficient metabolism. I could be stranded in a desert for three, possibly four, years with nothing to eat and maintain my body weight. And with a little effort I'm sure I could actually gain a pound or two. My metabolism knows how to shut down so quickly and efficiently that giving up any body fat is unlikely.

Exercise has never been something of which I'm particularly fond. In fact I hate it, pure and simple. I've never been athletically inclined. With this in mind, even I was surprised when I joined a health club. I wasn't smart enough to join one where I would find others like myself sweatin' to the oldies. No, I joined the gym where Hercules and Miss Universe prepare for their next competitions.

It took about twenty-one sessions with Trainer Jose, (TJ) before my sessions became something even closely resembling routine. The first habit I had to establish was remembering to show up.

I won't even try to convince you that it's been easy. It's been very, very, very difficult. Everyone around me at the gym seems to come by this weight-lifting thing naturally. Their well-cut, perfectly tanned bodies move in perfect grace and rhythm. I struggle with the most elementary routines, not unlike a baby elephant trying to get its balance.

Some time into my quest to fit in as a regular at the gym, TJ decided to switch my appointments to early morning rather than my usual evening schedule. I don't think I've had the opportunity to tell you that I am *not* a morning person. How much of a morning person am I not? If forced to an upright position before the hour of 7:00 A.M. I have a pounding headache, queasy stomach, puffy face, crabby disposition, and overall defeatist attitude. I feel very sad and can cry at will. Believe me, it's not a pretty picture.

Twenty-one may be the miracle number for other habits, but to think it could make me do morings was unbelievable. TJ assured me the morning schedule would be temporary. Even so, I kicked and screamed, whined and complained. The only reason I considered giving it a try was that my sessions for the following month had been prepaid. As precious as my sleep is to me, I preferred losing it to losing my money.

I made it to my 6:30 A.M. appointment several times. But as a happy person? One with the ability to say even one civil word? Not on your life. Just ask TJ, one of God's most patient creatures.

I was miserable and made everyone around me miserable. That was four months ago. Working out in the morning became such an unpleasant and impossible expectation that I quit. I quit the gym and I quit TJ. Habits are all fine and good, but some things are just impossible.

I went three weeks with no workouts; and as God is my witness, the most incredible thing happened. I realized that going to the gym and working out under the strong (and I do mean strong) arm of TJ had become a habit. It just didn't feel right not to go. I missed it and began to feel miserable. I had this nagging sense that if I missed twenty-one times the misery would go away and I'd slip back into my old habits.

The irony was that I, the sleeper-inner of the century began waking up earlier. It was not automatic but I noticed a definite change. A new habit was forming even though I'd been fighting it tooth and nail!

I rejoined the gym and rescheduled with TJ, who informed me that if I wished to return he would expect me to arrive at 5:30 A.M. (Ugh!) It's still not easy, but it's getting better.

Since the time I rejoined the gym, I've plotted out twenty-one morning sessions on my calendar. I'll reach that goal in two weeks from this writing. And guess what?

(You'll never believe it.) I've begun waking up without an alarm clock. I actually pop out of bed, have my wits about me, fly down the freeway, and arrive—not only on time but early. I'm able to carry on a civil conversation, and it has been enjoyable to witness TJ's reaction to this gradual change. Three times in a row I've arrived at 5:20 A.M.! Now, if that doesn't prove the twenty-one-day miracle, nothing will.

Should you ever see me walking down the street, think kindly. I will never have an athletic build, and I've just about decided that a thin one is not in my future, either. But I can curl some amazing poundage and am getting the hang of lunges and squats. I'm not half bad on the treadmill, and my resting heartbeat is becoming a much more respectable number. I've come a long way toward reaching my goal of being as physically active as possible until the moment God decides it's time for me to go.

Oh, by the way. Since my original donut experiment, I've reapplied the formula to the problem. It worked. And continues to work now many years later. Not only have I not eaten a donut since I cannot remember, I don't even think about them anymore. And when I do, like right now, I really have no desire to break my habit. For me staying away from donuts is a good thing.

This technique can be used to establish new habits such as balancing your checkbook, ceasing to use credit cards, establishing a daily program of skin care, making your bed, or walking the dog.

In the following chapters we'll be checking out nine behaviors of financially confident women. By choosing to mimic their behaviors consistently and over a period of time, you, too, can become a financially confident woman.

I am your constant companion,
I am your greatest helper or your heaviest burden.
I will push you onward or drag you down to failure.
I am at your command.
Half of the tasks that you do you might just as well
turn over to me and I will do them quickly and correctly.

I am easily managed, you must merely be firm with me.
Show me exactly how you want something done;
After a few lessons I will do it automatically.
I am the servant of all great people
and the regret of all failures as well.
Those who are great I have made great.
Those who are failures I have made failures.

I am not a machine but I work with all of its precision
plus the intelligence of a person.
Now you may run me for profit or you may run me
for ruin. It makes no difference to me.
Take me, train me, be firm with me and I will lay
the world at your feet.
Be easy with me and I will destroy you.
I am called Habit.

AUTHOR UNKNOWN

PART THREE

Nine Habits of the Financially Confident Woman

SIX

The Financially Confident Woman Is a Giver

To tithe is to trust. It is to acknowledge that God will provide, that God will protect. When you give to God you create an investment in your own spirituality, your community, your family and your faith.

JUDITH BRILES

There are three kinds of women in the world: Those who take, those who give, and those who keep dividing the world into categories. And while I have no statistics to support my contention, it seems to me the takers outnumber the others by at least a million to one.

While a person's propensity to be a taker or a giver may be an inborn characteristic not unlike any other personality trait, our society has certainly validated the takers and possibly converted many of those prone to be naturally-born givers, as well.

Take credit cards for instance (not literally, please). My credit cards offered me entitlement—the right to possess goods and services up to, and often over my allotted limit. To my mind, it seemed that the merchandise in stores was already mine, and I couldn't rest until I'd bought it and taken it home. The "have it all now" mentality has created a generation of takers, people who demand rights to which they feel entitled. No wonder this world is so out of whack.

Next time you have the distinct pleasure of vegging out in front of the TV for an evening, make a mental note of how many of the commercials have this underlying theme: *You're entitled to take all you can get.* If it's not a new luxury car that will define to the world who you are, it's a credit card that will guarantee you peace of mind and elevate you to a position of status you never thought possible. (How do they get away with such outrageous claims?) And the message commercial TV sends the kids of this country? It's frightening how they are subtly encouraged to get and take until their every little desire is fulfilled.

Learning to be a giver is probably the most important habit you can learn in your quest to become financially responsible. Being a generous person, one whose giving is so habitual it is almost automatic, will bring balance not only to your finances but also to your life. Giving provides the firm foundation upon which to build all the other habits we're going to erect.

I can't say I actually understand how giving works—how it is that in giving we receive. I don't understand how computers work either, but I've gotten into the habit of depending on the fact that they do. The work my computer so capably produces certainly makes me a believing nonunderstander. The same is true of giving. I don't understand it, but I believe in its power because the results have brought me indescribable joy and happiness.

There is something about the act of giving that cannot be explained in purely rational terms. I believe with all my heart that the act of giving invites God's supernatural intervention into our lives and our finances. I don't know about you, but the idea of opening my life to that kind of power is too awesome to miss.

Let me make this one thing perfectly clear: The attitude is not I-give-so-I-can-get. No way! What could be more manipulative than giving ten bucks on Sunday because you desperately want a hundred on Friday?

Giving back to God a portion of what He's given to us is an act of worship, gratitude, and obedience. It's always been that way as it always will be. Anything more than a no-strings-attached, no-expectations manner of giving is manipulation pure and simple.

The concept of giving somehow escaped me as a kid. Sure I knew about the concept on a purely intellectual level. I didn't, however, see the act for what it really is. I never caught the spirit of giving. Quite frankly, I figured God didn't really need my piddling amount of money. When I got really rich, when I got my finances straightened out, *then* I'd do some serious giving. I'd make a big splash with my philanthropic activities. What a dreadful, self-centered, self-serving attitude. But even with my arrogant attitude, God didn't stop loving me. He just waited patiently until I messed things up so badly it looked as if there were no way out.

In the truest sense of the word, I believe that by withholding what truly belonged to God I was in some way stealing from Him. Now that's a pretty horrible thought.

The very nature of grace is giving. God offers us grace, not because we deserve it or could possibly earn it, but simply because He loves us. Isn't is ironic that the credit card industry has picked up on this thing called grace? They offer what is known as a grace period. It's that time between a purchase and the time interest starts accruing. During the twenty-five-days or so, grace is extended in the form of "no interest due." Grace—it is a beautiful thing.

I give to God because I love Him and because I am grateful beyond belief for all that He has done for me every day of my life. Giving from a grateful heart and expecting nothing in return is a sweet offering to the One who owns everything I have anyway. It's the very least I can do. And as I give I experience God's grace.

Do you have a secret little problem with greed? Give! Is it tough to make the money last as long as the month? Give! Are you fearful of the future—afraid you will run out of resources, financial or otherwise? Give! Do you somehow feel your success and personal identity are tied to the balance in your checkbook? Give! When you are the neediest is when you should give the most.

How much should you give? Well, how much do you want to be blessed? You decide. Traditional thinking from ancient times until now says that ten percent is a good number. I like that and feel it is a good goal to set; but for heaven's sake, if you can't start with 10 percent, start with *something*.

Where should you give? Good question. You need to be a good steward of your gifts, so a bit of research on your part would be highly recommended. I suggest that if you are part of a church you should support it financially because that is the place where you are fed spiritually. When considering other charitable organizations or ministries, first request a current financial report. Learn what they are doing, how they do it, and who is in charge. Personally, I am suspicious of any organization that is not open with financial affairs and one whose overhead and administrative costs exceed 25 percent. In other words, at least seventy-five cents of every dollar I give should make it to the cause to which I've donated.

If you've never been one to habitually give, get ready to experience a whole new dimension in your life. I don't know of anything that will take your eyes off your own situation faster than giving to others. I am so excited for you because I know what will happen in your life when you learn the habit of generosity. If you want your life to have purpose, your finances to come into balance, and your faith increased, become a giver!

I would strongly suggest you add this to your personal belief system: *Part of everything I have is mine to give away.* If you really believe that, your attitudes will begin to reflect it, your behavior will change, and your life will be greatly enriched.

You may be tempted to brush this belief aside thinking that in order to give you must have an independent source of money. Every woman, whether single, married, or divorced, has some money that comes into her life, something over which she has control. It may not be a lot and it may arrive sporadically, but the principle still applies. I firmly believe that as we prove ourselves to be responsible with our resources, more and more resources will be entrusted to us to handle faithfully.

Quick Tips

1. Even though giving is best done in secret, share with one other person, such as your spouse, a friend, or a mature child, about your commitment to giving.
2. Make giving your first bill. If you can't start with ten percent, start with one percent and increase it each month. Make payment coupons and place them in the front of your bills-to-be-paid file.
3. Give away a percentage of your second most-treasured commodity: your time. Volunteer at a local shelter, food kitchen, hospital, or church. Visit several such organizations and ask God to direct you to the place your talents can best be utilized.
4. Be a responsible steward. Learn about the organization or individual who will be the recipient of your

charitable contributions. Ask questions about how much of each dollar donated actually goes to the use for which it was received.

5. If giving doesn't immediately produce a burst of joy, don't worry and don't stop. Remember it's easier to act your way into a feeling than to feel your way into an action. If you wait for the feeling before you start being a giver, you may wait forever. Ask God to make you a cheerful giver. The joy will come, I promise.
6. Each day ask God to show you little ways you can be a giver, even if it's simply holding the door for another person or assisting someone with his or her struggles. Once you catch this whole attitude of giving, confrontations on the freeway cease to be confrontational, irritating sales clerks don't seem so obnoxious anymore, and daily chores like laundry and carpooling take on a different meaning.
7. Copy Malachi 3:8–12 onto a card and post it where you can't help but read it every day.

I'm so proud of you for the decision you've made to invite God's supernatural intervention into your life. God will honor His promises! Your step of faith will be rewarded. Just keep expressing your faith in this manner and giving will become a lifelong habit.

Doing Things in Secret

Sometimes, the most important things that are done are done anonymously. For instance, I know of a man who loves to use his money to provide help for people who will never know who he is. On one occasion, I told him about a student of mine at Eastern College who was hoping to be a minister but was going to have to drop out of school because of lack of funds. This man contacted the college treasurer and arranged to have the bills paid. That student became one of the best preachers in my denomination. Hundreds of people have become Christians under his leadership. Thousands of lives have been influenced by his sermons. He never did find out who put up the money to keep him in school, but he often reminds me to tell that man of his gratitude. Behind it all there was a person with resources and the desire to do something that would live on after he was dead.[1]

Value:
Giving is an expression of my gratitude, a drain for my greed, and the way I keep my life in balance.

1. Tony Campolo, *Who Switched the Price Tags?* (Dallas: Word 1986), 65.

SEVEN

The Financially Confident Woman Is a Saver

The magic of compounding interest is truly
the eighth wonder of the world!

ALBERT EINSTEIN

Friends invited us for dinner one cold winter night. (In California, cold means you might want to consider a sweater.) The time of year and warm friendship blended perfectly with a dinner of homemade soup and honest-to-goodness homemade bread. I can say, without any doubt, that was the most delicious bread I've ever eaten. I had to have the recipe.

I soon learned I would need more than the recipe. I needed "starter," which looked as if it should have been discarded long before. The instructions were clear: *You must feed the starter every three to five days, at which time you must also take out one cup of this weird-looking stuff to make bread.*

It was fun at first, making homemade bread every three to five days. In a few weeks I became distracted and busy and had time to feed my starter but no time to make the bread. So I split and fed and ended up with two starters in the refrigerator. And then in five days I had to feed both of them, and remove one cup of the concoction from each starter and either make two batches of bread or do the split action again. My family of starters quickly began to take over the refrigerator.

Soon I became nearly obsessed with finding enough bowls and loaf pans to get all this bread baked because I didn't want to waste any of the precious starter. Visions of Lucy and Ethel in the chocolate factory kept coming to mind.

We had a lot of bread those first few weeks. However, it wasn't long before it completely slipped my mind to feed my brood of hungry starters. You've probably already guessed the outcome. I killed 'em.

This "Friendship Bread" is a wonderful idea. The way it's *supposed* to work is this: You occasionally give a loaf of bread to a friend along with a supply of starter (there's plenty to go around, believe me) and the recipe, which in an act of friendship starts the whole process of feeding, growing, baking, feeding, growing, baking in someone else's kitchen. I calculate that about six months of this process, if followed impeccably, could fill every refrigerator in the northern hemisphere with the goofy-looking stuff that has the unique ability to make one feel terribly guilty for not baking bread every three to five days.

It is a lovely plan, provided you follow it. You have to give away the right amount, you have to feed it, and you have to make sure you never use it all. You must always leave some in the refrigerator to grow for the future.

Which leads me (you knew I'd get there sooner or later) to saving money. Both money and Friendship Bread require that a delicate balance be maintained. You have to give some away, you must keep some to grow for the future (you dare not hoard the stuff), and you must use a good deal of it.

When it comes to finances, here's the bottom line: You can't keep it all, but you can't use it all either. *The key is balance.*

I have to tell you it makes me excited to know what's going to happen in your life once you're convinced that a savings program is something you must have. And personal confidence? You'll gain more than you could have ever imagined.

Correct Distribution

Here is how your money, whether it's your own paycheck, the household income, or retirement resources should be dispersed: Pay God first, pay yourself second, and pay others third. Take all the time you need to pick yourself up off the floor. Yes, you read it right. God first, yourself second, and others third. That's just the opposite of the way most people handle their money, paying everyone under the sun first and then having nothing left for God or personal savings.

If the goal is to give 10 percent of everything to God, and it is, why not dignify yourself with an equal portion? *Ten percent is yours to keep.* That sounds good, doesn't it? Yours to keep. Not to save for a new sofa (an excellent tactic for purchasing a new sofa, by the way), not to spend on next summer's vacation, but yours to keep. Yours to plant for the future. Yours to nourish and develop so that it will begin multiplying and working for you.

The Fringe Benefits

Saving money is its own reward. However, it has additional fringe benefits. Saving money is probably the best antidote for overspending. Saving money quiets the I-have-to-have-everything-now monster that runs so many of us ragged. It settles our spirits because knowing we've done the financially responsible thing by not spending all of our resources has a calming, quieting effect.

Saving money will bolster your attitude and give you the strength and courage to face the temporary sacrifices that may be required to get your money life straightened out. You see, once you have put aside some money, even if it's a fairly small amount, cutting back on groceries or temporarily giving up your weekly nail appointment becomes a choice you make rather than a cruel mandate over which you have no control.

Three years before we were able to rid ourselves of leased cars, we discovered that my leased car with two years remaining on the contract was worth about the amount of the remaining lease. The idea of selling it, paying off the lease, and sharing one car between the two of us made economic sense. But even the thought was pretty tough for me to swallow. I'd had my own car since my early twenties, and I enjoyed the independence it gave me. I was nervous about giving that up and worried it would feel like failure, like we were losing ground rather than making financial progress. Being hung up on status symbols and impressing outsiders is not given up easily.

We kept talking about it, writing down the numbers, and projecting how such a move would bring us that much closer to being debt free. Carpooling to the office we share would present no problem. But what about my speaking schedule? One car would never do on those occasions when we needed to go in opposite directions.

We made the decision to sell the car, determined to try the one-car arrangement for awhile. If it didn't work, we'd deal with it when the time came. In the meantime we agreed that I would rent a car when I had a local speaking engagement. That plan has worked very well for us. It's kind of nice to be chauffeured to work each morning, and I like driving a variety of brand-new cars when the need arises for a rental.

The best thing about the decision to go with one car after twenty-three years of having two between us was that we had a choice. By the time we made this car decision, we'd begun a regular saving and investing program. We were regularly putting away money that is growing for our future. We could've cashed something in or depleted an account to have the money to pay cash for a second car. Knowing we had choices made us willing to consider the most severe of the options.

But I know myself. If we'd had no money in the bank, giving up my car would have felt horrible, not like the choice that it was. It would have screamed "financial failure!" in my ears, and I'm afraid I would've done anything to not give up that car including incurring new debt or some other defeating tactic. I would have looked at it as a husband-imposed repossession, and you know where that would've led. Straight to resentment and disharmony.

The Miracle of Compounding Interest

I guess you've already gathered that accounting and finance were never on my list of career considerations. Let me put that another way: Math makes me break out in a rash. I barely got out of beginning bookkeeping. I'll never know why I actually selected that class let alone stuck with it. I don't like to think about numbers, formulas, axioms, postulates, or anything that is even remotely related. Believe me, no one was happier than I with the invention of the personal calculator.

In spite of being numerically challenged, I find compounding interest fascinating. I'm in good company too. Albert Einstein once declared the magic of compounding interest to be the eighth wonder of the world. And then there's Alvin Danenberg, another really smart guy who's also pretty wild about compounding interest. Al, a practicing periodontist and a registered investment advisor, has written a wonderful little book in language I not only understand but thoroughly enjoy. He explains compounding interest this way:

> In 1492 Christopher Columbus decided he was going to save for retirement. He had one penny ($0.01), and he knew he could earn 6 percent every year on his money. He put the penny in his left pocket and placed the interest ($0.01 x 6% = $0.0006) into his right pocket for safekeeping. He never added anything to his original penny in his left pocket. Yet, the interest accumulated year after year in his right pocket.
>
> Chris is a very healthy guy: He lives until today, 1996—504 years later—and exactly one year ago he decided to retire. So he took his one penny from his left pocket and added it to the simple interest in his right pocket. Do you know how much Mr. Columbus had?
>
> Well, the interest in his right pocket added up to only $0.30 (504 years x $0.0006 = $0.30). Along with his original penny from his left pocket, he has $0.31 on which to retire. Not very good planning!
>
> What could Chris have done differently? Let's assume Chris was much more astute about investing because he knew about compounding. Instead of putting the interest in his right pocket, he put it into his left pocket with the original penny—the principal. Over the years he would earn the same 6 percent interest on the original penny and the accumulated interest in his left pocket.
>
> As the story goes at the end of year 1, he had $0.0106 in his left pocket (the original penny plus the 6 percent interest). At the end of year 2 he had $0.011236 ($0.0106 plus 6 percent interest). At the end of year 3 he had $0.01191 ($0.011236 plus 6 percent interest). This is called compounding and continued for Chris for 504 years. How

much did good ol' Chris finally accumulate for retirement?

The answer is somewhat more to Chris's liking. At the end of 504 years of compounding the original penny at 6 percent interest, Chris has $56,774,862,806 (that's 56 billion, 774 million, 862 thousand, 806 dollars!). That's a lot of pocket change.

None of us will live that long, but all of us will have more than one penny to invest and will have the ability to compound our investments at higher rates of return.[1]

When it comes to interest, compounding simply means earning interest on the principal *and the interest* that you earn and then earning interest on that interest plus all the interest that you've earned on the principal and on and on.

There is nothing wrong with multiplying your assets by saving and investing. In fact, I believe that is the sign of a wise steward who obeys God's financial principles. You might remember the story Jesus told in Matthew 25:14–30. One of the characters in the story was given five talents to invest. He invested so well he multiplied the talents from five to ten. Another had two talents and doubled the value of his investment to four talents. However, the third took his one talent and buried it so it would be safe.

When the master of these three men returned he praised the first two employees for their wise multiplication through the investment of their resources. However, the third chap told the master he was fearful so he buried the money instead of putting it to work. The master

1. Alvin Danenberg, *21½ Easy Steps to Financial Security* (Chicago: International Publishing, 1995), 50.

called him a wicked, lazy steward who at the very least should have put the money in the bank where it could have earned interest.

Meet my fictional friends Sally and Jane. They're both the same age, and in this illustration they are committed to saving $600 a year which is, as you know, $50 a month. Sally is pretty smart and decides to start saving while she's quite young—at age twenty. Sally will save $600 a year for eight years ($600 x 8 years = $4,800) and then leave it alone and let it grow. Jane, a bit of a procrastinator, takes eight years to get her act together and doesn't begin saving $600 a year until she's twenty-nine. Jane contributes to this savings account a total of $22,200 ($600 x 37 years = $22,200) but cannot come close to catching up with Sally. The difference? Sally started saving early. Just further evidence of the magic of compounding interest.

Age	Sally Saves		Jane Saves	
21	$600.00	$660.00	0.00	0.00
22	600.00	1,386.00	0.00	0.00
23	600.00	2,185.00	0.00	0.00
24	600.00	3,063.00	0.00	0.00
25	600.00	4,029.00	0.00	0.00
26	600.00	5,092.00	0.00	0.00
27	600.00	6,262.00	0.00	0.00
28	600.00	7,548.00	0.00	0.00
29	0.00	8,303.00	600.00	660.00
30	0.00	9,133.00	600.00	1,386.00
31	0.00	10,046.00	600.00	2,185.00
32	0.00	11,051.00	600.00	3,063.00
33	0.00	12,156.00	600.00	4,029.00
34	0.00	13,372.00	600.00	5,092.00
35	0.00	14,709.00	600.00	6,262.00
36	0.00	16,179.00	600.00	7,548.00
37	0.00	17,798.00	600.00	8,962.00

AGE	SALLY SAVES		JANE SAVES	
38	0.00	19,578.00	600.00	10,519.00
39	0.00	21,535.00	600.00	12,231.00
40	0.00	23,689.00	600.00	14,114.00
41	0.00	26,057.00	600.00	16,185.00
42	0.00	28,663.00	600.00	18,464.00
43	0.00	31,529.00	600.00	20,970.00
44	0.00	34,683.00	600.00	23,727.00
45	0.00	38,151.00	600.00	26,760.00
46	0.00	41,964.00	600.00	30,096.00
47	0.00	46,160.00	600.00	33,765.00
48	0.00	50,777.00	600.00	37,802.00
49	0.00	55,854.00	600.00	42,242.00
50	0.00	61,440.00	600.00	47,126.00
51	0.00	67,584.00	600.00	52,499.00
52	0.00	74,342.00	600.00	58,409.00
53	0.00	81,776.00	600.00	64,910.00
54	0.00	89,954.00	600.00	72,061.00
55	0.00	98,950.00	600.00	79,927.00
56	0.00	108,845.00	600.00	88,580.00
57	0.00	119,729.00	600.00	98,098.00
58	0.00	131,702.00	600.00	108,568.00
59	0.00	144,872.00	600.00	120,085.00
60	0.00	159,360.00	600.00	132,754.00
61	0.00	175,296.00	600.00	146,689.00
62	0.00	192,825.00	600.00	162,018.00
63	0.00	212,108.00	600.00	178,880.00
64	0.00	233,319.00	600.00	197,428.00
65	0.00	256,650.00	600.00	217,830.00

SALLY'S TOTAL CONTRIBUTION: $4,800, JANE'S TOTAL CONTRIBUTION $22,200
(Note: Figures based upon 10 percent interest compounded annually)

The moral of this story? Start early and feed your savings plan often. The longer your money has to grow the harder it will work for you and the more productive it will become. In our example Sally contributed only fifty dollars a month for eight years. Jane, who snoozed for those first eight years, had to contribute more than four times as much principal than Sally, and she still ended up behind by nearly $40,000 at retirement!

How to Get Started Saving

First you have to plan ahead. If saving a specific amount of money at a specific time each month or week is something you don't do presently, you have to learn to treat your savings commitment no less mandatory than you do your rent, mortgage payment, or telephone bill. As long as you see saving as optional, your chances for success will be so-so at best.

Let's say you decide to save fifty dollars a month. To determine how much you need to save from each paycheck or other source of income, start with the annual amount (in our case it would be $50 x 12 = $600) and then divide by the number of times you are paid during a year. If you're paid monthly, it would be 12 times, weekly, 52 times; biweekly, 26 times; semimonthly, 24 times. Here's a quick example of how much you would have to save from each paycheck in order to have a $50-a-month savings plan.

- If you are paid monthly: $50.00 from each paycheck
- If you are paid weekly: $11.54 from each paycheck
- If you are paid biweekly: $23.08 from each paycheck
- If you are paid semimonthly: $25.00 from each paycheck

For some, saving $600 during the coming twelve months will be a real stretch, for others a drop in the bucket. I want to encourage you to be reasonable in setting the amount you will save on a regular, scheduled basis.

There's nothing magic about $50, its simply a suggested place to start. Saving 10 percent of your income is the goal we're going to shoot for, and the closer you can come to that in the beginning, the sooner you'll reach it. The plan is for you to start saving and then increase the amount you save regularly until it reaches the optimum of 10 percent. If you can't handle $50 a month to begin? Make it less, but start somewhere. I suggest you make the amount just slightly more than what you think is comfortable. I want you to feel this the same way you feel it when you work out.

Make a commitment that whatever amount you select you will save that same amount at the same time every month and that you'll not decrease it. Ever.

Finding a Parking Place

In the beginning, and especially if you've never administered your own savings program, I suggest you "park" your savings in a safe place.

Investment or financial professionals would undoubtedly define *safe* a little differently than I. They would want your money safe from inflation and loss of interest. I want your savings to be safe from you. Look, I know how we are. For example, keeping my savings in my underwear drawer is not safe because borrowing it back is all too easy. By safe I mean putting your savings in a place that is physically distant and very inconvenient. I can't tell you the number of letters I've received that have recounted the same scenario: *I started a savings account but this or that came up and I had to use it.* That's what I want to help you prevent.

The first step to safety is to open an interest-bearing account at a bank or credit union outside your local area. Pick a bank in another city, or if you really want to do something with great significance, open your account at the Tightwad Bank, Rt. 2, Box 204, Tightwad, MO 64735, (816) 477-3393. Opening an account and making deposits can be handled through the mail. Call me crazy, but the very act of writing out a check or money order to the Tightwad Bank is so goofy, it's the kind of thing that would keep me focused and amused at the same time.

Savings Coupons

Once you've determined the amount, frequency, and destination of your savings, make out your own custom payment coupons including the due date and minimum amount to be paid. If you will be depositing through the mail, make up a supply of stamped and addressed envelopes as well. Now is the time to create all the convenience you can think of. Keep these coupons and envelopes in the front of your bills-to-be-paid drawer. Once you have everything all ready to go, you won't be as likely to forget who's second in line to get paid. Exciting, isn't it?

Automatic Savings

By far the easiest way to save money is to have it automatically withdrawn and deposited into savings before you ever see it. Automatic savings can be set up with your employer or with your bank.

Many larger employers have a wonderful incentive program in which your savings are withdrawn from your paycheck before taxes (which means you'll pay less in taxes). And many employers will match what you save and then put the money into an investment program. These kinds of savings plans have different names, such as 401(k).

Here's how these savings programs work: You direct your employer or your bank to automatically withhold from your paycheck or withdraw from your checking account a specific amount of money. You might instruct your bank to transfer $50 from your checking account into your savings on the fifteenth of every month. The principle is: If you don't see it, you don't miss it. I know that sounds rather ridiculous, but it is absolutely true. In a short period of time, you'll not only not miss the money, you'll often forget all about it. And when you get just a bit too comfortable? It's probably time to increase the amount.

Creative Ways to Stash More Cash

Not everyone has a regular source of income or control over the family income. If this is true for you, making savings coupons or authorizing automatic deposits may not be possible at this time. So are you off the hook? No way! There are many other ways you can start saving. Here are some ideas to get your creative juices flowing.

Save All Your Change: This is probably the most painless way to sock away an additional couple hundred bucks each year. When going through the checkout stand, even if your bill comes to $4.02, don't break out the two cents. Hand the clerk a five and you'll end up with ninety-eight cents in beautiful change to deposit into your change jar. When it gets full simply wrap the coins and make a savings deposit. Harold taught me this trick. He can't stand to carry around change and has a change receptacle in the car, one in his desk, and another on his bureau. His all-time great change year netted him $1,100, and those were after-tax dollars.

Keep a bank in the laundry room: The way I see it, she who does the laundry keeps the cash. How do those coins and bills make it through the wash and dry cycle, anyway? Unless your family is highly neglectful, your total take won't be much, but every little bit counts. I find at least $25 a year in the laundry.

Give Up Expensive Habits: If you spend just $5 a day eating breakfast or lunch out, you're spending $1,270, a year; and that's allowing for two weeks of vacation.

Eating at home or carrying your lunch two days a week will allow you to save at least $500 in the next twelve months. Imagine what you could save if you quit smoking, gave up lottery tickets, or cut back on other expensive habits you support.

Save All Refunds: Instead of cashing rebates and refund checks, save them. Take your grocery-store coupon savings in cash. Next time you shop, ask the checker to give you the subtotal before coupons are deducted, write your check for that amount and then ask for your coupon savings to be given you in cash. Stash the cash in a special place or savings account, and you really will be saving money by using grocery coupons.

Hang On to Windfalls: As you receive unexpected sums of money, such as gifts, bonuses, inheritances, retroactive pay, awards, and dividends, don't cash them, stash them. If you put those checks into your regular checking account they will just be absorbed into your everyday living expenses. Instead deposit them—no matter how small—into your savings program.

Keep Making Payments: As you pay off a credit card or other loan, keep making the same payments, but instead of sending them to the lender, put them into your savings account.

Save Reimbursements: When you are reimbursed for travel or other out-of-pocket expenses, save the money instead of putting it into your checking account where it will just disappear.

Sell Assets: It's a pretty sure bet all of us have far more stuff than we really need or can possibly appreciate. Just think of everything you have to keep track of, protect, clean, store, insure, and worry about. Have you ever considered how much freer you might feel if you got rid of all the clutter and stuff that is nonessential or fails to bring joy and beauty to your life? What would you gain by unloading things that are robbing you of so much freedom? Sell! Liquidate! Give your savings program a jumpstart with the proceeds.

QUICK TIPS:

1. Make savings your second bill. Once a month when you pay your bills write a check to deposit in your money market fund or savings account. If you can't start with ten percent, start with less and increase the amount each month. Use automatic savings plans. You won't miss what you don't see.
2. Give up a bad habit. Save money and maybe your life too.
3. Save your change at the end of the day. Small amounts add up quickly. Put all coins in a jar at the end of the day and decide to stop spending change.

Value:
Part of all the money that flows into my life is mine to keep; and I pay God first, myself second, and others third.

EIGHT

The Financially Confident Woman Is an Investor

Money is like an arm or a leg—use it or lose it.

HENRY FORD

You don't need to have an extraordinary income or spectacular education to become a successful investor. Take the story of one Ohio gentleman. Years ago he, a typical blue-collar worker, became outraged by what seemed to be unreasonable utility rate increases. It's easy to understand how helpless he felt as he saw more and more of his paycheck going to keep lights burning in his modest home. It angered him when he thought of how rich those utility company owners were becoming off his meager wages.

As the story goes, our hardworking middle-class fellow decided to show them a thing or two. Because his utility company allows customers to own shares of stock in the company (most utility companies do), he decided that each month when he paid his electricity bill he would write out an additional check equal to one day's wages. With this second check he would purchase shares of ownership in the company. He figured if he couldn't beat them, he'd join them. As the years went by he faithfully carried out his commitment, always making that second check equal to his current daily rate of pay.

I've been told that this man became the second largest stockholder in the company and a millionaire many times over. Now he was not a rich man when he began buying stock. On the contrary, by his peer's standards he was probably on the low end of the spectrum. But he practiced the two cardinal principles of effective saving and investing: He invested a predetermined amount of money at a set time of the month, and he stuck with it. Little by little his money went to work for him so that he was able to achieve financial security. According to Al Danenberg, financial security is *that point in time when you can live the lifestyle you have chosen, financed from the assets you have accumulated, without the need for any additional income.*

There was a time in my life I really believed a person needed something in the neighborhood of two thousand dollars to start a real investment program. Of course we just never happened to have an extra couple of thousand dollars lying around, so that was our excuse for not starting an investment program. I paid little attention to the fact that I didn't have a clue how to get started anyway, so a lack of cash allowed me to remain in my state of investment ignorance.

But take it from me—one of the world's most mathematically challenged individuals, a woman who experiences total brain fade at the mere mention of investment terminology—you need not have a college degree or a lot of money to become an investor. What you do need is a sense of purpose, a healthy dose of determination, eyes that see beyond the moment, and a library card. The fact that you are a woman with inborn ability to nurture and protect makes you a natural at this investment game. You'll know when the time is right to make that leap from saver to investor.

Saving is the simple process of amassing money. Other than earning small amounts of interest, saving is an inactive process. Saving means never having to expose money to risk. Of course you don't expose it to reward, either.

Investing means to put money to use by purchase or expenditure in something offering profitable returns. Investing is an active and dynamic process. Investing implies a willingness to accept the prospect of risk in order to achieve even greater rewards. Investing is not synonymous with gambling or wild speculation. A wise investor always holds the safety of her investment dollars to be of the utmost importance.

Rules of Beginning Investing

There are three simple rules when beginning to invest:

1. Do not get into anything you do not understand.
2. Do not get into anything that is not immediately liquid (turned into cash easily).
3. Do not allow an outsider to control your investment or make investment decisions for you.

Several years ago I challenged myself to start a respectable investment portfolio with just twenty-five dollars. I'd heard somewhere this was possible. Frankly, it sounded about as likely as turning dryer lint into Persian rugs, but I decided to check it out anyway.

I shuffled through periodicals and investment books; and after nearly giving up on the idea, I came across a great book for beginning investors that gave me confidence I could accomplish my goal.

I decided that a no-load, growth mutual fund was the investment vehicle I would choose for my maiden voyage. I must confess I wasn't really clear just what all of that meant, but I felt confident enough to proceed. What did I have to lose? Twenty-five dollars is important, but I could drop that in five minutes at the grocery store without looking back or being concerned. Surely I could put the same twenty-five at risk in the world of investing without losing sleep.

What Is a Mutual Fund?

Picture this. You have a couple dollars and you decide you want to buy stock, which, simply put, is a tiny piece of ownership in a large company.

You call your local friendly stockbroker and place your order for twenty-five dollars worth of, let's say, IBM. You are laughed off the phone because not only will the brokerage not handle such a small transaction, twenty-five dollars wouldn't even purchase one-half of a share of IBM stock; and by the time you'd paid the hefty brokerage fee (sales commission), you'd find this transaction completely unrealistic.

You decide to get together some of your friends (naturally I'm one of them), acquaintances, and relatives and convince everyone to join you in your investment by putting a couple bucks into a common pot so that the group has enough to buy IBM stock without putting more than twenty-five dollars of each person's money into the pool. Now we have two hundred dollars to invest. We've created a *mutual fund*.

None of us knows exactly what to do next. Someone mentions a friend named Florence who might be willing to help us out. She knows about this kind of thing, and everyone agrees to appoint Flo to pick out some stock for us to purchase. We now have a *fund manager*. We don't want to put all our investment into one company, so we agree to purchase shares of several companies. In case we make a bad choice we won't lose all our money. Now we are *diversified.*

Flo, being a savvy business woman, says that she wants five dollars for her trouble. If we agree and pay her the fee, we'll have $195 with which to buy stock. Our fund now has a *load* (commission to Flo) on the *front end* (before the stock is purchased). A restless murmur ruffles through the group and we decide to change Flo's compensation. No one likes this commission thing, so we decide to let Flo be part of the group and own a small part of the fund but she won't have to put in cash. Now our mutual fund is *no-load.*

To keep everything straight we decide to write down some rules for the group in case anyone has some extra money next month and wants to buy some more ownership in our mutual fund, or if someone needs their money back, etc. This is our *prospectus.*

Flo makes excellent choices, and at the end of the first year the stocks pay dividends (which would be similar to interest in a different kind of investment) and go up in value. The group decides to instruct Flo to buy more stock with the dividends instead of divvying up the profit between us. Now we have *growth.*

Take the foregoing example, multiply the number of participants and contributions by several zillion, throw in heavy duty laws and federal regulations, give Flo hefty academic degrees, some new clothes, and many years of investing experience, and we have a no-load, growth mutual fund. Simple as that.

Look, Learn, and Invest

Back to me and my twenty-five dollar investment program. In March 1993 I made my initial purchase in an aggressive no-load, growth mutual fund (meaning this particular fund invests in riskier stocks). I selected this fund for a variety of reasons, not the least of which is I plan to invest regularly for the next twenty-five years. I will add at least the same amount of money at the same time every month without fail. I figure some months I'll buy when the price is down and other months the price will be up. But overall, I believe it will average out to my benefit. This is called *dollar cost averaging.* I filled out the proper paperwork so that my monthly deposit is made directly from our checking account. It's easy; and in these three years, this particular investment has done very well.

To be perfectly candid, I go months without even thinking about it and that's the way it should be. Investments of this kind should be made for the long haul and not hovered over. The stock market has regular peaks and valleys, and to watch it on a daily basis could drive someone like me over the edge.

In addition to this particular mutual fund, Harold and I now own many such investments. One at a time we have researched and made our decisions based upon understanding. If we don't "get it," we don't invest. Not all of our investment dollars go into the riskier vehicles such as stocks and mutual funds. We've learned from the experts how important it is to have a strong, safe base for our *investment portfolio* (which simply means all our investments collectively), so we've purchased savings bonds and other types of treasuries (which are backed by the full faith and credit of the United States government) and bank certificates of deposit.

Please understand, I am not an investment counselor and certainly not qualified to recommend how you should invest your money. All I can do is encourage you to learn for yourself and then make wise and informed decisions.

I promise you this: If you will take the time and exert the effort to learn, you will be rewarded.

Four Characteristics of Successful Investors

Successful investors possess these four characterisics:

1. Successful investors have a plan, and they stick to it.
2. Successful investors invest regularly.
3. Successful investors are patient.
4. Successful investors do not "marry" their investments.

In the Resource section at the end of this book you will find a list of books including several on beginning investing. These are my favorites and from which I've learned the most.

I have a good idea that once you get going you're going to love this new challenge called personal investing. You might even want to consider starting or joining an investment club.

Quick Tips:

1. Never be ashamed to invest small amounts.
2. Add to your investments on a regular basis to take advantage of dollar cost averaging.
3. Don't hover. Watching your investments on a daily basis will drive you nuts. Just keep feeding them and let them grow.

Value:
I invest my money in ways that make good sense to me, utilizing investment vehicles I understand.

NINE

The Financially Confident Woman Doesn't Do Unsecured Debt

Those who borrow are slaves of moneylenders.

PROVERBS 22:7

My first encounter with the word *debt* was in 1959. The Lord's Prayer—and its reference to forgiving debt—was part of the Get-Your-Way-Paid-to-Summer-Bible-Camp-by-Memorizing-Thousands-of-Verses Contest. Anyone who could successfully rattle off every single verse on the long list was awarded the coveted week at camp. To me, understanding the principle of *debt* in that context was about as pertinent as the drying time of paint. Qualifying for the trip was all that mattered.

I ran into a derivative of the word *debt* in my high school bookkeeping class. Mr. Black attempted to teach us the difference between debits and credits.

The theory of debt again crossed my mind (briefly) when I applied for a college student loan. A loan with payments deferred until some more convenient time in a far-off decade seemed so benign, so manageable. With my future at least four times longer than my past, why on earth would I let debt become of any concern at my tender age of eighteen?

By the time I hit thirty-something I'd experienced firsthand the phenomenon of being able to buy now and pay later, and quite frankly I'd found it to be neither easy nor something that brought satisfaction for any significant length of time. You might say I'd formed a love-hate relationship with consumer debt, and the love part was all but dead.

I allowed debt to creep into my life and wrap me in its tentacles. Believe me, it was trying its best to choke me to death. That's when I finally saw debt for what it truly is—a seemingly harmless little friend with a bent toward deceit and the unique ability to grow into an all-consuming monster.

Financially confident women do not feel prohibited from using credit, but I can assure you that they never think of debt as normal or commonplace. On the rare occasion they take on debt, it is well thought out, for a very short period of time, and because they have a sure way to make full repayment.

True, credit has become quite commonplace in our modern society, and there is no doubt it's here to stay. The problem is that far too many of us have become strangled in our own credit lines. Debt has a unique ability to destroy wealth, damage relationships, and dispel joy when it ceases being a tool and becomes a noose with which we hang ourselves.

The Truth about Debt

Debt Is Easy to Get Into

Never before in the history of this country has credit been so available and debt so attractive. A bank credit card is available to most anyone who can show as little as $14,000 annual income. While it is no longer lawful for credit card companies to send unsolicited credit cards through the mail, preapproved applications have become as common as any other type of junk mail. These applications can be as simple as a form requiring only a signature or as surreptitious as a large check made payable to the recipient that when endorsed activates a new line of credit complete with transaction fees, hefty interest rates, annual fees, and an instant monthly payment.

With an estimated 95 million American families in possession of more than 720 million credit cards and five hundred new issuers scheduled to launch their cards before the year 2000, we haven't seen anything yet when it comes to easy credit card availability and slick marketing. Silly as the thought might be, the free prize packed in your kids' favorite breakfast cereal may turn out to be their first credit card—an idea that may not be all that far-fetched given the way credit is taking over our society.

The emergence of new players in the credit card market means there's going to be more competition to retain you as a customer and to get you to sign up for new cards. You are a valuable commodity to credit card companies, but don't be too flattered. They have anything but your best interest in mind.

The average nonthinking person views an approved credit application as a badge of honor, a sign of having arrived, and concrete proof she or he is certainly able to handle this amount of debt. Nothing could be farther from the truth. The credit card issuer sees you as a risk worth taking in order to increase their profit margins. They are banking on the fact that you will charge a decent amount of debt, habitually pay only the minimum monthly payment, and never be able to pay the balance in full. Fitting into that profile and operating according to their highest dreams and expectations makes you nothing more than a pawn on their chessboard of high finance.

Debt Is Expensive

Would you intentionally take more than thirteen years to pay back a $3,000 loan at 17 percent interest if it meant that you would end up paying more than $2,650 in interest alone for the privilege? Probably not. But that's what happens when you choose to make low minimum monthly payments offered by the typical revolving credit card. And the ugly truth is that few people run up a balance of three thousand dollars and then stop incurring new debt during those thirteen long years it takes to pay it off, one pathetic minimum monthly payment at a time.

Don't think for a moment that the credit card companies accept such a small portion of the actual amount owed each month out of the goodness of hearts or as an act of friendship. They're no fools!

The amount you are required to pay as a minimum each month (usually 2 to 4 percent of the outstanding balance) is actually the credit card company's profit—the interest you pay as a privilege of borrowing their money. If you pay off your entire balance each month, they've lost their golden-egg-laying goose. Ironically, cardholders who pay on time are known among industry insiders as "deadbeats" because they aren't paying their share of interest.

The credit card companies make sure they get their money every month. By allowing you to roll the entire principal over to the following month, they're pretty much assured you'll stick with them for a long, long time. *Perma-debt* is what they call it, and that's what supporting a megabillion dollar industry in this country, an industry growing by leaps and bounds.

At midyear 1995 the amount consumers owed on VISA, MasterCard, Discover, and the American Express Optima cards crossed the $300 billion mark for a total of indebtedness of approximately $315 billion, representing a whopping 26-percent increase over the past twelve months. Consumers have been going deeper into debt at the rate of more than $5 billion per month or about $173 million per day![1]

I don't know about you, but it's difficult for me to even *think* in terms of billions. One of my *Cheapskate Monthly* readers, Ed Boden, sent me a bit of trivia that helped me understand the immensity of a billion or even a trillion dollars, which is how we now measure our national debt: A dollar bill is about 0.0038 inch thick. A stack of one thousand bills is about 3¾ inches high. Ten thousand bills would be 1½ inches more than a yard high. A million would be 12½ feet higher than a football field is long. A stack of a billion bills would be 59.2 miles high, and a trillion would be 59,186 miles high. Our national debt at $4.77 trillion would make a stack of one-dollar bills 282,000 miles high! The moon is nominally 239,000 miles away, so our national debt in dollar bills is about 43,000 miles beyond the moon. The same analogy can be used to visualize one's personal debt. It takes $3,200 to make a one-foot stack of dollar bills.

But wait—there's more! Just like the Ginsu-knife dealers, our friendly credit card companies have something special to throw in, something designed to keep their finest customers loyal to the bitter end (and yes, for many the end is very bitter). For those who struggle along month after month and manage to make their minimum credit card payments on time, an award is awaiting—a little something to brighten the spirits and lift the

1. *CardTrak of America, Inc.*, Issue #55, August 1995.

soul: a credit-limit increase! And just as company executives hope, most cardholders look upon that letter announcing the increased amount of money available as a trophy suitable for framing, proof of a job well done. Credit card companies absolutely love those who play the game according to their rules.

Geraldine, a divorced mom of three teenagers, works full-time and has qualified for a $7,500 loan from her credit union. Getting this loan will allow her to take care of some house maintenance she's been putting off, will cover the cost of a much-deserved vacation—a cruise sponsored by a ministry she supports, and will leave her with a little cash cushion in case of emergency. She will be charged 16 percent interest over sixty months, and her monthly payment will be $182.39. Given her present financial situation she concludes that even though it will be a stretch she will be able to cover the payment on her present salary.

Unfortunately Geraldine made no further inquiries before signing for the loan. The monthly payment was her only concern. But let's take a look at the full price tag—the real cost for Geraldine to borrow this money. In addition to repaying the initial $7,500, Geraldine will have to pay $3,443 in interest for a total repayment of $10,943. But that's not all. In order for Geraldine to come up with the $10,943 necessary to repay the loan she will have to earn considerably more because she will pay the loan with after-tax dollars. You forgot about that, huh? So did Geraldine.

In our example let's say Geraldine is in a 15 percent federal tax bracket, must pay 7.65 percent social security/Medicare taxes, and lives in a state with 7 percent state income tax. That's a total of 29.65 percent that will be taken right off the top of Geraldine's earnings. So in order to pay back the $10,943 in principal and interest, Geraldine will have to earn over $15,565 in gross income. That is Geraldine's full price tag for a $7,500 loan. More than twice the original loan amount. Amazing, isn't it?

A better alternative would be for Geraldine to force herself to make $182.39 payments into the Bank of Geraldine, putting the money into an interest-bearing account for a little over three years. That's how long it would take her to save the $7,500 cash.

Debt Can Be Dangerous

Debt can be dangerous for your wealth, your marriage, your relationships, and your peace of mind. It's not so hot for your blood pressure, either. Statistics tell us that around 70 percent of all divorces found their roots in financial difficulty. I'm not saying that money troubles cause all divorces, but it's the money issues that get the conflicts going.

In the past year, for some reason I've not yet figured out, I've received letters from people who are serving time for embezzling money from their employers. The stories are all so similar it's spooky. Invariably it goes like this: *The debts were so huge, the bill collectors so nasty, the family relationship so fragmented, I had to do something. I only took a small amount at first, but it was so easy. So I took a little more and it just got out of control.* I received a letter from a husband-and-wife team who were serving simultaneous sentences because they'd both become involved in breaking the law to deal with their debts.

The Magnitude of Debt

Debt is not a pleasant thing. Unsecured debt like credit card bills, installment loans, and personal loans is the worst kind. At least if you buy a house, which is a secured or safe debt, and it turns out to be more than you can handle, you have the option of selling it, paying off the loan, and moving on to something else. Not so with unsecured debt. The very fact that the debt is unsecured means there is nothing of value being held to guarantee payment of the loan.

There was a time in my life that I regularly carried a very large and equally heavy handbag. So heavy was my bag, it turned out to be the cause of severe shoulder and neck problems. I've reformed in this area; and I now carry a tiny little thing just big enough for keys, lipstick, identification, and money. What a difference!

Carrying debt is a lot like my heavy handbag. It is cumbersome and a constant burden. Taking on additional debt would be like adding a shoulder bag, and then a backpack, and another bag for the other shoulder. Now if these heavy bags are debts, using a credit card to pay the credit card bill would be equal to tucking three or four bricks into each bag. Just picture yourself struggling through life, carrying all this weight. It's very difficult to get anywhere or make any progress, but the worst part is how difficult the journey is. Trying to stand upright with all this weight is nearly a full-time job. There's no time to look up and see the beauty, to experience the joy of the journey. While others who are less encumbered pass you by, you can't help but envy their ability to take side trips and excursions. But can you go? No way. You can't just dump the burdens in the trash or hope someone else will pick them up for you.

And when you pass through the struggles of life such as sickness or unemployment, those debts don't magically disappear. No way. They're heavier than ever. While it's hard to imagine, there are those (I know because I hear from and about them) whose debts become so unbearable suicide appears to be the only alternative.

Debt destroys options. When burdened with debt you give up the option to quit a job in order to return to school. Or leave a miserable job to take one that pays less but would allow you to do something you truly love. Debt prevents us from following our dreams, or following our heart's desire to serve God in some profound way.

I'm reminded of the young woman who felt God was calling her to teach in a missionary school abroad. However, her debts were so large there was no way she could quit her present employment. She had no resources from which to pay the debts and so she had to turn down the opportunity to go where she believed God was calling.

Each time you increase your debt you eliminate more options. The reverse is true too. Each time you reduce your debt or pay another one off, you get back more options, until the day you are debt free and your options are at an all-time high. That's what I call freedom!

Appropriate Credit Card Use

The following guidelines will get you into the wonderful position of having a credit card work *for* you instead of against you.

1. Every family probably needs one credit card. Make sure it is one with no annual fee and a twenty-five day grace period. The interest rate should be of little consequence since you will never pay interest, ideally.
2. Never carry a balance over from one month to the next. If you cannot pay the balance in full during the grace period (usually twenty-five days after purchase, during which time no interest is assessed), you have no business placing a charge on the card.
3. Do not carry the credit card with you. Instead keep it in a safe place with your other important papers. Most people have plenty of notice that they will

need to rent a car or secure a hotel reservation. For most of us, carrying the card with all its buying power is too tempting.

4. There's only one thing you can do with two credit cards that you can't do with one—incur debt!

A word of caution. Many credit card companies these days are using all kinds of gimmicks such as cash rebates, frequent-flier miles, gasoline, and U.S. savings bonds to entice us to use their cards and use them often. On the one hand, I would suggest that if you are a responsible credit card user (meaning you pay the entire balance during the grace period), why not get any perquisites available? But be careful. At about a penny per mile, you'll need to charge a lot of purchases in order to end up with anything close to an airline upgrade or "free" trip. Same goes for the cash back and gasoline. It's all bait. The credit card companies are hoping you get hooked on all the "freebies" and finally start letting your balance roll over from one month to the next.

Don't Be Fooled by "Low Monthly Payments!"

For some reason I get tons of mail-order catalogs. Usually I flip through them just to see what they have. However, a catalog from a major mail-order company caught my attention recently. Even though I knew the company was notorious for selling inferior merchandise at steep prices, what I saw appeared to be a departure from their previous modus operandi. Imagine a nine-piece set of nonstick cookware for just $12.79. Or how about a twenty-four-piece bath-towel ensemble for $10.79?

I knew there had to be some kind of printing error because these prices were way too good to be true. I have no idea how long I perused this merchandising phenomenon before I figured out the scam. All the prices printed were the "low monthly payment." When I multiplied the monthly payment by the number of payments required and added in shipping and handling, these items became among the most overpriced goods on the planet. How dare they be so deceitful, hiding the truth in the tiniest of print in an obscure place in a language barely resembling English? I suppose they would argue they met the standards they are required to follow. The only solution is that the buyer must always be careful to avoid this kind of consumer debt.

Pay-Off Plan

If you are presently in debt, carrying balances from one month to the next, consider setting up your own rapid debt-repayment plan. It's not difficult and you can customize a plan that fits your situation perfectly. The first step is to make a commitment to not incur any new debt while undergoing this repayment plan. That may be difficult, but it is absolutely necessary.

Next, you must pay more than the minimum amount due each month. If you absolutely cannot increase the amount you are presently paying, concentrate on just one of your debts while paying the minimums on the others. Once you get that first debt paid off, use its payment to make larger payments on the next debt you concentrate on. You will be amazed how quickly you can pay debts off once you are determined and focused. (You can find a detailed plan for setting up this kind of plan in chapter 11 of *The Cheapskate Monthly Money Makeover*. See Resources at the end of this book.)

Let's say you're paying your bills next month. Finances are very tight, and the thought enters your mind that, while it's not much, you could increase the regular payment on one of your debts by five dollars. But then another thought quickly replaces that one: *It seems so insignificant. Why bother? That five dollars won't make a bit of difference in the long run, but I could certainly use it to buy lunch tomorrow.* That is a myth, a lie, a total falsehood. Prepaying principle in any amount is always an excellent move.

Take a look at the following table. The first entry shows a $1,000 debt accruing 17 percent interest with $15-a-month payments. It will take more than seventeen years to pay that loan at that rate. And look at the total payback required for a loan of $1,000. Wow! The next entry illustrates the overall effect if the monthly payment is increased by only five dollars per month. Only five dollars a month more drops nearly ten years from the total payoff time and saves nearly $1,200 in interest. Remarkable!

How Much Difference Can Five Bucks Make?

Balance	% Interest	Monthly Payment	# of Payments	Total Payback
$1,000	17	15	205.5 months (17 yrs., 1 month)	3,082.50
$1,000	17	20	87.5 months (7 yrs., 4 months)	1,750.00

Quick Tips:

1. Cancel all but one all-purpose, no-fee credit card to be used when you need to rent a car or reserve a hotel room. Accept a credit limit which you could easily pay

in full on your present income. Reject all credit-limit increases.

2. If you ever use your one card, pay the balance in full during the grace period.
3. Avoid credit-repair clinics or "specialists" who make promises to solve your credit-report problems. There is no lawful way to repair a bad credit report or remove a bankruptcy from your file. Don't pay them a nickel.
4. If you are in debt, commit to getting out as quickly as possible.
5. Never pay your credit card bill with a credit card!

Value:
Living on credit keeps me locked in the past.

TEN

The Financially Confident Woman Lives beneath Her Means

Living beneath your means is the only route to take to enjoy a secure and comfortable standard of living throughout your working and retirement years. Living beneath your means isn't a suggestion. It's an imperative. Spend less than you earn!

JONATHAN D. POND

Any woman with a lick of fashion sense knows the secret of style is found in three little words: accessorize, accessorize, accessorize.

Men have it easy when it comes to accessories. All they have to worry about is a tie, a watch, a belt, and maybe a briefcase. Their shoes don't really count as accessories because they're almost always the same color and height.

But women? We have to deal with earrings, watches, bracelets, rings, necklaces, belts, chains, brooches, scarves, glasses, stockings, socks, hair ties, clips and bows, headbands, handbags, briefcases, and shoes of every style, height, and color. Being properly accessorized is anything but cheap. Or easy.

First it's a matter of finding suitable storage space. Now I've observed individuals who appear to be wearing every accessory they own, but we usually need lots of space to store all the accessories not currently in use. Proper arrangement just screams for some type of time-consuming, fancy organizational system because, as they say, If you can't find it, why have it? Or as I used to say, If you can't find it, replace it.

However, in an amazing fit of sensibility several years ago when I discovered the loss of yet another piece of ear jewelry, I made a rash decision. From that moment on I would own just one all-purpose, lovely pair of earrings. I would wear them all the time. Period.

Why not? I thought. I wear the same ring day after day, year after year, and have not yet been arrested for taking unacceptable fashion risks.

At the time, I didn't realize what a brilliant decision this was. This small change simplified my life immeasurably. I've saved all kinds of time not having to decide which earrings to wear. And even more time not having to locate two that make a reasonable match. Because I always know the exact location of my one pair of earrings, I haven't lost one of this original pair in four or five years. And that represents a sizable monetary benefit.

Ironically, this idea born out of a desire to stop spending so much money on earrings has produced an even more desirable fringe benefit. Simplifying, even in the tiniest ways, makes my life more enjoyable. Simplifying helps reverse the process of being overpowered, overextended, overworked, and overcome by the pressures of life—pressures that are mostly self-imposed.

Simplifying, even when done in a tiny way, has the ability to refresh the soul. You won't believe all the extra time and freedom you'll enjoy, to say nothing of the positive effect on your bank account.

Living simply doesn't mean moving back to the land, ditching your favorite appliances, or slaughtering your own meat, unless of course that's your idea of simplicity. Simplifying means reducing scale while maintaining comfort, eliminating complexity whenever possible, and minimizing the time demands that have a way of devouring us.

Here are a few tips for simplification that might work for you. Perhaps they'll help you think of other ways you can slow down and enjoy the things that really matter.

- Stop buying clothes that need to be dry-cleaned. Maybe you prefer to spend fifteen to twenty dollars a week running to the dry cleaners, but just consider the expensive waste of time it represents.
- Make water your drink of choice. Just think of all the cans, jars and bottles you won't have to buy, lug home, and then lug back to the recycling center.
- Sell the stuff. If you've reached the point where you no longer believe the bumper sticker, "He who dies with the most toys wins," it's time to start unloading. Author Don Aslett hits it right on the head when he says, "Dejunking is the cheapest, fastest and most effective way to become physically and financially sound, emotionally and intellectually happy."[1]

There's only one way to accumulate money. You must have more money coming in than going out. You have to make more money than you spend. You must spend less money than you make. This is a simple principle, and those who live according to it know the result of spending less than you earn is financial security. If you spend it all, there will be nothing left over. And if you spend *more* than you earn, you're on the road to trouble with a capital *T.*

1. Don Aslett, *Clutter's Last Stand* (Writer's Digest Books, 1984).

Affluent people are those who earn money and manage to hang onto it by spending less than they make. Frugality is one thing that separates the affluent from the rest of us.

Perhaps the terms *frugality* and *thrift* cause you to grimace. I know that's how they affected me. The words meant nothing short of purchasing my entire wardrobe at a thrift store. No way was I ever going to buy my clothes at the thrift store, a promise I made to myself at age eleven. Guess that tells you where many of my clothes came from.

I plead with you to give up your biased ideas of what frugality means. Just give it a chance. I believe you may come to learn that being frugal and living with thrift in mind are actually virtuous characteristics. You need not fear becoming one big fashion disaster or less classy and dignified than you are right now. I have confidence in you.

When you think about it, there is little we actually *need*—that is, really need in order to sustain life. These needs of course would be shelter, food, and clothing. These things are absolutely essential to sustain life. The next level of expenses are certain comforts we've come to enjoy and want in our lives. And finally there are luxuries, those things in which we indulge to pamper ourselves.

The ideal way that our finances should be distributed is this: 10 percent to be given away, 10 percent to be saved, 80 percent to live on—to cover essentials, comforts, and luxuries. Not easy if you've been used to living on 100 percent, or more, giving little if any and saving nothing.

Frugality simply means striving to get the very best value you can for each dollar and fully enjoying the things you have or make use of.

Frugality is not an activity reserved for the poor and underprivileged. Instead it is a noble way of life that is to be admired. To approach life with a mind toward frugality is to celebrate life, to surround oneself with beauty, and to be content. Living a life of frugality offers a giant sigh of relief to those of us used to overconsuming and underenjoying.

We are so wasteful of the abundance that comes into our lives and our homes. Right living means using things up, wearing them out, and even doing without now and again. To be frugal means to have a high joy-to-stuff ratio. It means balance, not having too much or too little but just the right amount.

Think of all the stuff in your life, a great deal of which you probably haven't used or even thought about in years. If it isn't truly useful or doesn't bring beauty and joy to your life, why have it? Think of all the things that take up your time and energy because they need to be dusted, polished, fueled, mowed, insured, secured, and fussed over.

There's something refreshing about simplifying, about knowing when enough is enough. Both the Old Testament, "Don't let me be too poor or too rich. Give me just what I need" (Prov. 30:8), and Jesus when he said "You cannot serve both God and money" (Matt. 6:24), challenge our culture's adage that more is better and you better get all you can right now.

Cut Back in Every Area

The key to reducing is to look at the whole picture. You probably do not need to eliminate one area entirely, but rather cut back a little bit in every area.

Once you've kept a written spending record (chap. 11) for one or two months, you will have no problem seeing where the money goes. And you will know instinctively where the cuts need to be made.

As you look at your first full month of recorded spending, play with the figures a little bit. Muster all the courage you can and multiply some or all of them by twelve. It's good to see what you will spend on fast food, for example, if you continue spending at your current rate. Or the telephone bill. We fool ourselves by never thinking about total annual costs. Spending sixty dollars a month for telephone service may not seem like much, but that's $720 in one year. If you could reduce that bill by 30 percent (not difficult if you apply all the cost-cutting techniques available) you will realize a $240 savings in a one-year period. That's remarkable.

By now you've rethought your values, particularly those related to money. Focus on what you've determined is really important in your life and the lives of your family members. We get so caught up in our lifestyles we fail to realize we're spending a great deal of our money on things that don't even fit into our value system.

Seventy-seven Ways to Spend Less Money

General

1. Give up the myth. Myth: Buying things on sale is a great way to save money. *Truth:* Buying things on sale is a way to spend less money, but it has absolutely nothing to do with saving money.

2. Stop trying to impress other people. If you can stop spending according to demands put on your life by others (through peer pressure or the necessity to keep up), you will see a tremendous difference in the way you spend.

3. Stop shopping. To me, shopping means strolling through the mall with nothing particular in mind, simply looking for great bargains and things that happen to strike my fancy. That is a very dangerous thing to do. I'm not suggesting that you never again buy anything, but that your spending should become a planned act of acquiring the goods and services you need, not spur-of-the-moment, impulsive spending.

4. *Anticipate.* There's nothing more frustrating than waking up in the morning to a water heater gushing forth water from a rusted-out bottom or a flat tire with the steel belts exposed. You have no choice but to replace them immediately. Now, had you anticipated the tire was about shot or the age of the water heater meant you were on borrowed time, you could have watched for sales and had time to comparison shop. But you've no choice but to get whatever you can by any means possible. And you will invariably spend a great deal more, especially if you have to make that purchase on credit.

5. *Purchase with cash.* Retailers are keenly aware of the statistics that prove you will spend at least 30 percent more if you are in the store with a credit card, debit card, or checkbook. The last thing they want is a customer who carries cash. Why? Because they know how cautious and nonimpulsive the cash buyer is.

6. *Keep a spending record.* Seeing where your money goes keeps you from lapsing into a spending coma.

7. *Save first, spend later.* Instead of putting larger purchases on credit, save first. Once you have enough cash, make the purchase. Amazingly, by the time you save up the money, you may change your mind a dozen times. You might even decide you no longer need or want it.

8. *Combine errands.* Instead of running all over town several days a week, combine all your errands into one trip.

9. *Buy used if at all possible.* Buying used items costs less, the price is usually negotiable, you usually avoid sales tax, and it provides a counterbalance to the spendthrifts and obsessive "upgraders."

10. *Use baking soda.* It's cheap. As a non-abrasive scouring powder, it cleans and shines chrome, unclogs drains, removes hard-water marks, cleans plastic, removes odors, degreases, removes stains from marble, cleans fiberglass,

removes crayon stains from washable walls, and when added (½ cup per load) to laundry with liquid detergent it greatly improves effectiveness.

Your Car

11. Reassess transportation. Perhaps you don't really need more than one vehicle. Many cities have lovely public transportation facilities. Have you tried yours lately?

12. Pump your own gas. While most people already do this, there are some who still believe women are not capable of doing such a simple task. Learn how. You'll save somewhere between twelve and fifty cents per gallon. Multiply that out over a year's time and you'll be convinced.

13. Do it yourself. Take a course in basic auto repair to learn how to change your oil, oil filter, and antifreeze. Learn to spot a hose that needs to be replaced and detect the origin of a fluid leak.

14. Buy, don't lease. Generally speaking, leasing a new car is the most expensive way to go. Better: Purchase a late-model used car. The major depreciation of the car occurred during its first year when someone else owned it.

15. Keep your tires full. Check them weekly to make sure they're impeccably inflated, holding exactly the amount of air pressure as recommended on the sidewall of the tire. You should be able to increase gas mileage by up to 10 percent.

16. Keep your trunk empty. The more weight you're hauling around, the fewer miles per gallon you'll get from your fuel. So unload all that heavy stuff you've been carrying around. For the best performance limit your trunk's contents to the necessary safety emergency equipment recommended by the manufacturer in the owner's manual.

17. Locate a reliable and trustworthy mechanic. The best time to do this is before you need one. Get a recommendation from a friend, relative, or neighbor. A mechanic's reputation follows closely whether it's good or bad.

18. Increase your automobile insurance deductible. Check with your agent, but chances are excellent that if you increase your deductible to around five hundred dollars, you will receive a greatly reduced premium.

Food

19. Grocery shop with a list. A list is your game plan. Entering the store without it is flirting with financial disaster. The food industry spends some $6 billion a year to weaken your resistance with fancy packaging and compelling displays. Staying out of the store unless absolutely necessary will decrease your exposure time.

20. Arrive at the grocery store with cash only. You will become a much more careful consumer as a cash buyer. This is particularly helpful for the compulsive shopper who would rather stick toothpicks under her fingernails than go through the checkout only to find out she doesn't have enough money.

21. Be brand flexible. Staying loyal to a specific brand might be a noble endeavor, but it will cost you a lot of money in the long run. If you are willing to go with what's on sale and the brand for which you have a doubled coupon, you'll end up keeping more of your money.

22. Shop solo. Your concentration will be better if you leave the kids at home, and you'll get out of the store faster. And your kids won't fall into temptation purposely set by smart marketing organizations. On your next trip to the store, stoop down a bit and check out what's been strategically placed at the eye level of small shopping-cart passengers.

23. Shop at the cheapest store. Most cities have stores with prices that are consistently less. Shop there.

24. Purchase spices from a health food store. Many health-food stores offer spices in bulk allowing you to purchase as little or as much as you need. Prices? Just a fraction of the prepackaged version.

25. Think vegetarian. Once or twice a week prepare a meatless meal. Serve meat as a side dish or ingredient rather than the entree.

26. Make your own baby food. Experts agree there is no superior nutritional benefit to store-bought baby food compared to food made at home. It only rates high on convenience. Caution: Never substitute your own formula or rice cereal. These are the only exceptions. Use your blender to puree food, then place the food in ice-cube trays and freeze. Food cubes can be stored in zip-type plastic bags and thawed out as needed.

27. Use sale ads. Plan your meals and shopping list around what's on sale this week.

28. Stock up on sale items. If possible, buy enough when it's on sale to last until the next time it hits the sale sheet.

29. Coupons. Use them only for items you'd buy if you didn't have the coupon. Always buy the smallest qualifying size when using a coupon.

30. Double coupons. If you are a couponer, try to find a store that doubles their value.

31. Double milk's useful life. Simply add a pinch of salt to milk when first opened. This will retard bacteria growth but will not effect the taste.

32. Investigate store brands. Most grocery-store chains now have their own private labels. In most cases the product is the same as a name brand (usually packaged in the same plant) and labeled under the store's private name. The price is always less. National brands are priced higher because the costs of advertising must be added into the price of the product.

33. Weigh produce. Prepackaged produce must have a minimum weight as printed on the packaging. However, not all potatoes are created equal, so a ten-pound bag may weigh eleven pounds, and a one-pound bag of carrots may weigh 1.5 pounds.

34. Know your prices. Compile your own price book. List all the items you buy regularly, the regular prices of the stores in your area, and the per-unit price (per ounce for example). Now you will know if a sale is really a sale. Retailers are smart. They know if they put a display at the end of an aisle with a big sign announcing "Special," consumers will assume that it's a bargain. If you know your prices, you won't be fooled.

35. Buy in bulk cautiously. It's no bargain if you end up throwing some away because it spoiled before it could be consumed. Break down large quantities into smaller plastic bags that can be sealed or frozen for future use.

36. Out of sight, out of mind. This can work in your favor or against it. If it's a case of soda pop you picked up at a great price, hiding it under a bed might be a good way to keep the kids from drinking it all in one afternoon. On the other hand, a roast purchased on sale and slipped into the freezer could be forgotten for many months, at which time it might have spoiled. Enzymatic action is not arrested during the freezing period.

37. Buy in season. It takes a little research to know what's coming into season and what's not. Out-of-season produce is the most expensive. Stick to what's plentiful and therefore cheaper.

38. Expired doesn't always mean bad. Because of store policy many foods that are still wholesome are reduced in price when approaching their expiration dates. Many products reduced for quick sale can be a wonderful bargain. Ask the butcher and produce manager what's about to expire. Offer to take it off their hands provided the price is right.

39. Empty the pantry. Most of us have pantries and freezers full of stuff we don't even consider using. By being creative and building menus around what you already have, you might be able to increase the time between grocery-shopping trips. Every day you don't go in the place is another day you can't make an impulsive purchase.

40. Buy local produce. Typically, your local farmer's market will have better prices for far better products. But make a list and stick to it. A beautiful produce market can be as deadly as a beautiful mall. And produce spoils quickly. Buy only what you can reasonably consume.

41. Avoid convenience food. The closer you can stay to basic ingredients such as eggs, sugar, and flour (also known as cooking from scratch!) the less money you will spend.

42. Substitute, experiment. Many people worry about meticulously following the recipe, as if the slightest deviation could change their ambrosia to Alpo. Lighten up. If a recipe calls for a cup of bacon when you have leftover ham in the refrigerator, use the ham.

43. Join a membership warehouse club. Approach this tip with caution. Make sure you will save at least the amount of your membership fee. And get a grip on your impulsive nature or you could end up owning cases of stuff you really cannot use.

44. Eat lunch . . . for dinner. When eating out at dinner time ask to see the lunch menu, or request the luncheon portion of the item you select. Typically you will save 20 percent, with the added benefit of having a lighter meal and not overeating.

Banking costs

45. Don't bounce checks. With banks currently charging anywhere from ten to thirty dollars per occurrence, bouncing a check can have quite a punitive result. And don't forget the merchant who took your bad check may have a returned check charge that can be around twenty-five dollars or more. Bouncing checks can be financially deadly.

46. Find a free account. It may take some searching, but there are many banks that offer free accounts with a minimum balance.

47. Ask for free checks. Some banks give free checks, (don't expect anything fancy) if you ask. If you can't manage free checks at least buy your checks directly from a check printer like Current (800-533-3973) or Checks in the Mail (800-733-4443). You will save up to 60 percent of the price the bank charges.

48. Consider a non-bank. Credit unions are often better, cheaper, and safer alternatives for handling your money. Typically, credit unions are smaller, which allows for more personalized service. Credit unions are nonprofit organizations more interested in benefiting their memberships than amassing big profits, which is reflected in lower interest rates and fees, and generally have higher standards when it comes to qualifying borrowers and loan-to-deposit ratios. You need to qualify to join a credit union. Write to the Credit Union National Association, P.O. Box 431, Madison, WI 53701 to find out if there's a credit union you may be eligible to join.

49. Average daily balance. If your bank calculates your qualifying balance using the lowest figure of the month, you could easily get socked with some painful penalties should your balance dip down below the minimum even on one day during the month. Make sure your fees are determined by the *average* daily balance.

50. ATM Machines. Use only automatic teller machines (ATMs) that are networked into your bank's system and for which you will not be charged a transaction fee.

Utilities

51. Find the water leaks. Give your home this test: Turn off all running water in the house. Find your water meter and take a look. Is it still moving? Chances are you have a water leak and chances are even better it's your toilet. Put a few drops of food coloring into the toilet's tank. If without flushing the color shows up in the bowl, it's leaking all right!

52. Fix leaky faucets. A faucet leaking sixty drops a minute wastes 113 gallons of water a month. That's 1,356 gallons a year!

53. Use cold water in laundry. The bulk of your laundry is only lightly soiled. Modern-day detergents do just as well with cold as warm. Your colors will last longer too.

54. Experiment. You may be able to use as much as 50 percent less laundry detergent than recommended by the manufacturer depending on the properties of your water.

55. Install dimmers. Anything you can do to reduce the number of watts you burn will reduce your electricity bill.

56. *Select energy-efficient appliances.* Use the yellow energy guide labels to make your choices. These appliances consume less energy.

57. Use crock pots and pressure cookers. Electric burners, gas flames, and traditional ovens are far more expensive to operate than crock pots and pressure cookers. Anything that radiates heat wastes energy.

58. Plug money leaks. Take advantage of your community's free or low-cost programs for insulating your home.

Check with your utility companies or community action center.

59. Turn on to efficiency. Compact fluorescent light bulbs use one quarter the energy of incandescents. The initial cost is ten to fifteen dollars per bulb, but they often last ten to fourteen years while cutting your electricity bill by up to 40 percent.

60. Get out of hot water. You'll save heat and water in the dishwasher if you wash only full loads and choose the air-dry option. Don't prerinse dishes. Lower the water-heater temperature to 120 degrees and let the dishwasher do the rest.

61. Create body heat. Raise your body temperature one degree by wearing slacks instead of skirts. Light, long-sleeved sweaters add another two degrees of heat; heavy sweaters, four degrees; and two light sweaters, five degrees (due to the insulation layer of air between them). For extra warmth put on heavy socks with your slippers. Add a quilt to your bed.

62. Turn it down. In the winter keep thermostats set to sixty-five degrees by day and sixty degrees by night unless you are elderly, in poor health, or taking certain types of medication, in which case you should consult your physician.

63. Plug air leaks. Here's how to check for air leaks. Shut the doors and windows. Move a lighted candle around the perimeters of the door or window. If the flame flickers you have an air leak. Plug it with caulk and weather stripping.

64. Install a clock-operated thermostat. These are reasonably priced and will pay for themselves in no time at all in reduced heating/cooling bills.

65. Turn them off. Turn off electric stove burners and the oven several minutes before specified cooking time. The retained heat will keep on cooking.

66. Multiple dishes. When using the oven, cook several dishes at the same time. Use a timer and don't open the door if at all possible until cooking time is completed.

67. Check refrigerator seal. If it's loose, replace it. Cold air is probably escaping, causing the motor to run more.

68. Write postcards instead of calling. Unless you need to hear a voice, a simple postcard to the person can accomplish the same end as a long-distance call. And it's cheap—only twenty cents as of this writing. Keep a stack of postcards by the phone to remind you.

69. Call 800 Assistance. Before calling a company long distance, call 1-800-555-1212 to see if they have a toll-free number. Most businesses do.

70. Six-second billing. If your present long-distance carrier does not give you six-second billing (instead of billing the next full minute) you may be paying too much. Shop around and find a carrier that does. You could save 8 to 15 percent on your long-distance calling.

71. Telephone book. Directory assistance is no longer a free service. You may have a limited number of complimentary calls per month. Going over it will cost you a lot. Pick up the phone book whenever possible rather than calling information.

Entertainment

72. Movie switch. Instead of a movie and dinner, take in a bargained-priced matinee and dinner or dessert after.

73. Have potlucks instead of dinner parties. The ultimate no-obligation gathering where everyone brings a part of the meal is a great social occasion.

74. Escape to the library. You'll be amazed what fun you and your kids can have at the library. You can borrow videos, CDs, audio cassettes, and books-on-tape in addition to fabulous books. Some libraries have story time and documentary-film showings.

75. Go for a walk. Chances are you live in a neighborhood you've never explored up close and personally.

76. Write a book of your family's history. Let the kids write and illustrate their own personal chapters.

77. Hold a neighborhood kids' art fair. Display all the artwork and ask adults to purchase their favorites. Let children vote on which charity will receive the proceeds.

Value:
I can live comfortably and more simply
and still spend less.

ELEVEN

The Financially Confident Woman Is Prepared for Emergencies

You lazy people can learn by watching an anthill.

PROVERBS 6:6

Forgive me, but if I hear the following piece of financial advice one more time, I'm going to scream: "You need to have an emergency fund that should equal three to six months of your living expenses." And I *should* have a Rolls Royce and several ladies-in-waiting.

You know why that advice irritates me? Because of the period after the word *expenses.* Call me informationally needy, but how can anyone make that statement and not follow it up with exact "how-tos." After all, figuring out how to have thousands and thousands (and for some many, many thousands) of dollars available to pay for all of a family's living expenses for up to six months is no small feat—especially if you're drowning in debt without a dime in savings.

So what did we do when we were in that situation? Nothing. We kept going the way we were headed and figured if we couldn't have $50,000 or so in an emergency fund, we'd have nothing. The logic of that idea escapes me, but it seemed quite rational at the time.

Since my financial reformation I have come to look upon this matter of an emergency fund as wise advice. More than that, I believe it is absolutely essential if financial peace is to be achieved, and I've learned it is possible to make this seeming impossibility become reality.

Define Emergency, Please

You and I both know that for some of us "emergency" can mean anything from the midyear sale at Nordstrom to a 3:13 A.M. hospital trip. I used to operate much like the federal government. Once a situation was worthy of being declared an emergency, all limitations on spending were overridden. Christmas became an emergency. Perhaps you've experienced it: It's December 15, the kids are entitled to a great Christmas, which is measured, of course, by the number and size of gifts. We have no money. We call the credit card companies to plead for credit-line increases. Given the increases, we now feel authorized to run wild, to purchase stuff that will be forgotten before the bills arrive in January.

No, my friend. Christmas is not an emergency on our journey to financial confidence. When it comes to establishing a fund to handle it, *an emergency is the temporary loss of income.*

You probably know of someone, perhaps yourself, who has been in some way separated from their income. It can be due to a job layoff, a tragic disability, or any number of other reasons. The loss of one's income can be one of life's most devastating events.

Two Cases in Point

Tom and Lisa live paycheck to paycheck on Tom's salary. There's never enough money. They're habitually late with their bills but manage somehow to get caught up several times a year. Tom is able to work overtime during tax season, which helps a lot. However, due to downsizing at his firm, Tom is given a two-week notice of his scheduled layoff. Like a batter who's been "dusted" by an opposing pitcher, Tom and Lisa are knocked to the ground emotionally. What will they do? They're one month behind on the mortgage payment, both of their new cars are leased, and Lisa's made reservations for herself and the girls to fly to Florida next week to visit her parents.

They have no sources from which to draw. Tom hasn't been with the firm long enough to warrant severance pay. Their credit cards are maxed out, as is the equity in the house.

Lisa recalls that a preapproved line of credit from a big finance company came in the mail a few days ago. She madly rummages through the trash, finds it, and breathes a sigh of relief. At least they have $3,500. She decides not to bother Tom with the matter because the last thing he needs to worry about is more potential debt.

Tom spends the next two weeks putting together his résumé and sends out hundreds of copies with no particular rhyme or reason.

After eight incredibly long weeks, Tom finally gets his first unemployment check, but it doesn't begin to cover the stacks of bills growing on the table. Lisa is beside herself with worry, wishes she'd never gone to Florida, has gone through the $3,500 from the finance company, and is about to lose her mind because Tom spends every day pacing and stewing.

The first foreclosure notice arrives three months following Tom's layoff. Creditors call daily. Lisa's stomach is in a knot most of the time. She has one nerve remaining, and it's about shot.

Finally, after four incomeless months, Tom receives a job offer. It's not exactly what he'd hoped for and the pay cut will be hard to handle, but it's a job with a paycheck. He jumps at the offer and within two weeks receives his first, albeit smaller, paycheck.

It's been two years since Tom's job change. He's not that happy in this position but has decided to grin and bear it. Lisa has taken a part-time job at the kids' school and hates every minute of it. They've still not recovered from the devastation of the layoff. Their debts are higher than ever, and their credit report is all but ruined. Worst of all, they're no more prepared for a future layoff than they were before.

Greg and Jody have three children. Jody has a small desktop-publishing business in their home, and Greg is a foreman at the local steel plant. Greg participates faithfully in his company's 401(k) plan, contributing 5 percent of his gross pay into the fund, and the company matches his contributions. He's been doing this for years since he started at the plant during high school. In addition, another 10 percent is deducted and automatically deposited to their money-market mutual fund. Greg has been at the plant long enough to know that good times come and go. While the chances are fairly slim, he could be laid off. Even if it was temporary, he needs to know they have money set aside to cover the bills.

As a result of deep cuts in defense spending, Greg's company loses the government contract they had for many years. In no time at all, pink slips are distributed; and as you might have guessed, Greg receives his. While of course this is not good news, it is not devastating.

Greg spends the next two weeks dreaming and exploring options. He and Jody talk about all the things they've wished they could pursue but have rejected because of Greg's job.

They withdraw just the minimum amount needed from the money-market account to cover their basic living necessities during the time between Greg's last paycheck and first unemployment check. They also supplement the unemployment checks with their emergency funds to keep the bills paid and food on the table.

Greg puts together a résumé based on his dream of becoming a professional photographer. He includes information on competitions he's won as well as examples of his work. Over the following two months, he follows up every possible lead in the area of photography and lands not one, but two interviews.

Greg is offered a position as an apprentice with the largest commercial photography company in the city, and he eagerly accepts. The pay is quite similar to what he's been making at the plant, but it lacks the fringe benefits.

During the first year of Greg's new job, he and Jody are determined to reduce expenses sufficiently to allow for replacement of the money they took from their emergency fund. They increase the semimonthly contribution to 15 percent instead of 10 so as to repay it more quickly.

Greg and Jody did not have a negative reaction to their set of circumstances. In fact, Greg looks back upon the layoff as one of the best things that ever happened to him. This blessing disguised as a pink slip opened the doors for him to blend his life's work with his creative passions. They didn't miss a beat in paying their house payment and utility bills. Because they had the peace of mind an emergency fund can bring, they actually had fun during this unexpected time between jobs.

Tom and Lisa, on the other hand, suffered greatly. Their relationship was dealt a blow because Lisa activated that $3,500 loan without Tom knowing. Tom became so depressed Lisa didn't even want to be around him. The girls became needlessly fearful that they would be homeless. And each month rather than getting ahead they fell further and further behind as their debt grew and grew.

Tom is anything but fond of his job, but he feels hopelessly stuck. Lisa resents having to work, and it now looks as if she will need to find a full-time job in the fall. Tom's layoff has greatly altered their lives, and they are much worse off for it.

Establishing Your Emergency Fund

I'm sure that since you're still with me here, you're at least considering the value of establishing some kind of an emergency fund. First, face the facts regarding job and income security. Don't count on it. With technology increasing at a breakneck speed and the nation's economic system having more peaks and valleys than a rollercoaster, it's almost certain that sometime your income will at least temporarily be cut off. It's going to happen, so plan on it instead of being blindsided by it.

Start with baby steps. I agree that a figure equal to six months' income is rather overwhelming, paralyzingly so. Instead of focusing on that big number, cut it up into bite-sized pieces. How much would it take for you to live one week without income? Let's just assume that number is something like two hundred dollars. Now I'm not saying that would cover your house payment or rent, but two hundred dollars might be enough to keep gas in the car, food on the table, and the utilities paid.

Focus on saving enough money so that your emergency fund equals one week's living expenses. That is an achievable goal.

Your next step is to decide where to keep your emergency fund. Take it from me: that secret pocket in your handbag is not the place. Since this is going to be a little like playing the odds, chances are good the emergency fund will sit and grow for a long time. It might as well be earning interest. Each day, your emergency fund will be losing its purchasing power due to the heartbreak of inflation, so earning interest will help maintain the purchasing power of this money.

In the beginning your few dollars are probably just fine in your bank or credit-union savings account. As it grows and you accumulate something around two to five hundred dollars, you would be well advised to open a money market account. You will earn better interest. This type of account has a minimum that can be withdrawn (mine provides me checks just like a checking account with the stipulation that I cannot write a check for less than one hundred dollars).

Once you have a one-week emergency fund, enjoy having made this accomplishment. Let me congratulate you in advance. Now take the next step: continue adding to the fund until your fund is equal to two weeks' living expenses. Keep going until it reaches six. Since most unemployment benefits "kick in" about six weeks into the unemployment period, you'll have enough to survive that first interim period.

While it would be wonderful for you and your family to have an emergency fund separate from your regular savings program, that might be a bit aggressive in the beginning, especially if you've not had a savings program in the past. I would suggest you allow this emergency fund to accumulate and gain interest. Provided it is kept in a fairly liquid account (remember, even in the worst circumstance you will only need to get your hands on small amounts at a time) it will certainly qualify as an emergency fund and a very healthy savings program.

While my definition of an emergency fund is money held exclusively to replace lost income, you should establish your own definition. There may be times you need to pay a large insurance deductible because of a claim you've been forced to make (sounds like an emergency to me) or replace your roof or make some other major home or automobile repair. These may fall under your personal definition of an emergency. I, however, call them something else.

Irregular, Intermittent, or Unpredictable Expenses

Expenses that don't occur on a regular monthly basis are often forgotten. When they rise up to remind us of their existence we often refer to them as emergencies. They're also considered financial crises.

Irregular, intermittent, or unpredictable expenses would include things like insurance premiums, new brakes on the car, veterinarian bills, vacations, clothes, Christmas. They are expenses that don't occur at precisely the same time or the same amount every month, month after month.

My theory is this: Most of us have found a way to handle mortgage or rent payments, grocery bills, utilities, car payments—our monthly expenses. It's all the other things that creep up on us and scare us to death that send us running to the credit cards or some other form of credit. If we could just come up with a way to predict those expenses, we could plan ahead and never be caught off-guard again.

A wonderful tool which I've titled the Freedom Account is perfectly designed for being prepared for irregular, unpredictable, or intermittent expenses rather than being derailed by them.

Here are the basic guidelines for setting up your own Freedom Account.

1. Using a year's worth of check registers, credit card statements, and paid receipts, reconstruct the irregular, intermittent, or unpredictable expenses you had to deal with last year. These are things like medical

and dental expenses, taxes, insurance, vacations, and Christmas.

2. Annualize these figures (multiply so that you come up with a dollar figure for the year) and divide each by twelve. One-twelfth of each expense is what you need to set aside each month in anticipation of these ex-penses.
3. Open a separate checking account to handle your Freedom Account.
4. Each month deposit one-twelfth payment for each of the above items.
5. Set up a notebook with a separate page for each category or subaccount. Each month enter that month's deposit and calculate a new balance.
6. As irregular, unpredictable, or intermittent expenses come up for which you have set up a subaccount, write out a check from the Freedom Account to make the payment. Record it on the subaccount page as a debit, and calculate the new balance.

Used properly, the Freedom Account will revolutionize your finances. Being prepared for emergencies, large or small, is great all on its own, to say nothing of all the fringe benefits like less stress, more financial options and an overall feeling of maturity, responsibility and well-being.

> Ants don't have leaders, but they store up food during harvest season. How long will you lie there doing nothing at all? When are you going to get up and stop sleeping? Sleep a little. Doze a little. Fold your hands and twiddle your thumbs. Suddenly, everything is gone, as though it had been taken by an armed robber.
>
> PROVERBS 6:7–11

Quick Tips:

1. Start building an emergency fund with a reachable goal: an amount equal to one day's wages. Now increase it to equal your take-home pay for one week. Keep increasing until your emergency fund is equal to six months' income.
2. Keep your emergency fund in an interest-bearing account like a money-market mutual fund. Even in the worst case you won't need all of it at one time, so when the total grows sufficiently, consider placing part of it in a thirty-or sixty-day certificate of deposit. The point is that at least part of your emergency fund should be liquid, meaning you could get your hands on it within twenty-four hours.

Value:
An emergency fund is mandatory to keep me financially viable during those seasons when my cash flow is cut off.

TWELVE

The Financially Confident Woman Knows Her Financial Condition

Always do right.
This will gratify some people and astonish the rest.

MARK TWAIN

It doesn't matter if you're single or married, if you handle the finances in your home or not, every woman needs to possess certain basic financial skills that enable her to:

- balance a checkbook,
- prepare a Personal Financial Statement,
- develop a Spending Plan, and
- prepare a Cash Flow Statement

How to Balance Your Checkbook

If you think I'm going to start out by telling you this is easy, think again. Remember who you're dealing with. I'm the one who gets mathematics-induced rashes. I will tell you that once you've balanced your checkbook twenty-one months in a row (ah, the miracle of twenty-one), it will become a habit; and yes, I think you'll find it to be a fairly easy task and something you rather enjoy. Chances are very good, too, that it will not take twenty-one times. Think of it as intensive monthly housecleaning. It's not that much fun to do it but the results are worth it.

The reason you need to balance your checkbook once a month is so that you do not bounce checks. There was a time when bouncing a check wasn't that critical from a monetary point of view. But those days are gone. Not only is it extremely expensive to bounce a check (banks are charging fees up to thirty dollars per bounce—aughhhhh!), depending on how you receive notification that you're underdeposited several more checks could be bouncing; and then you really have a mess on your hands. A financially responsible woman does not bounce checks.

To me, the hardest thing about a checking account is remembering to write down the amount of a check as it is written. We found duplicate checks to be the solution. Each check has its own carbon copy record that remains in the wallet once you've pulled out the check. With this contemporaneous record, you will always know to whom and for how much you wrote each check.

Before you even start this reconciling procedure, make sure you have calculated a current balance in your checkbook that reflects all the checks you've written and the deposits you've made since the last time your account was reconciled.

To balance your checkbook assemble the following:

1. Your checking-account statement that comes monthly from the bank.
2. Canceled checks. (Some banks no longer enclose these with your statement.)
3. Your checkbook register or check stubs.

4. Checkbook Balancing Worksheet (found on p. 148).
5. Pencil and eraser.

Step 1. Place the canceled checks into numerical order.

Step 2. Look at the statement and compare the actual canceled check with the amount of the check as noted on the statement. Banks do make errors now and again. For instance, you might have written a check for $48.26 but the check shows up on your statement as $84.26. Circle or make note of any discrepancies.

Step 3. Go through your check stubs or register and check off each check that has been enclosed with this statement. If you have a stub or entry in your register for which you do not have the paid check in the statement, list that amount under "checks outstanding."

Step 4. Look on the statement for any bank charges, such as the cost of checks, service fees, or overdraft fees. Enter these bank charges in your check register and deduct the amount just as you would if you'd written a check for this amount.

Step 5. Look on the statement for automatic or direct withdrawals you may have authorized, such as insurance payments or investment transfers. Make sure these are deducted in your register just as if you'd written a check for that amount.

Step 6. Look for direct deposits (some people have their paychecks, dividends, or social security checks deposited directly, and some checking accounts earn interest). Make sure each has been entered into your check registry as a credit and added to the balance.

Step 7. Make sure you have entered every automatic teller machine (ATM) withdrawal into your checkbook and your statement doesn't have a few extra on there that

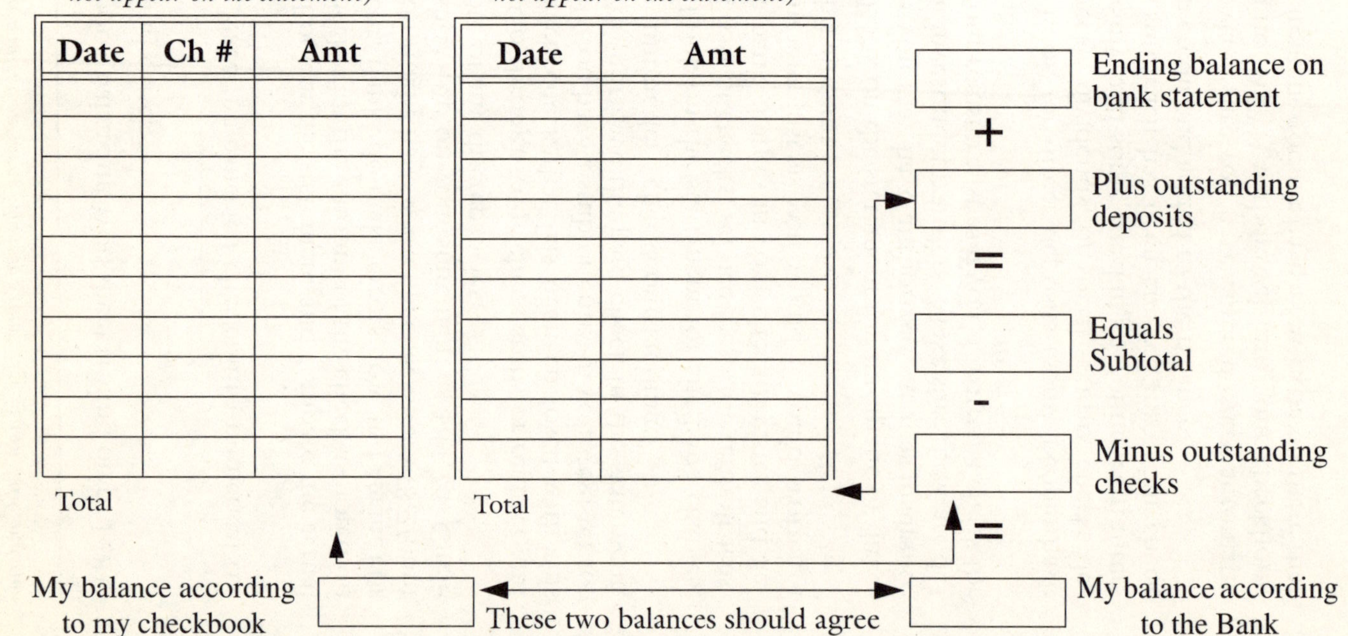

Worksheet for Balancing Checkbook

Month of ____________

Outstanding Checks
(Checks I wrote that do not appear on the statement)

Date	Ch #	Amt

Total

Outstanding Deposits
(Deposits I made that do not appear on the statement)

Date	Amt

Total

Ending balance on bank statement

\+

Plus outstanding deposits

=

Equals Subtotal

\-

Minus outstanding checks

=

My balance according to my checkbook

These two balances should agree

My balance according to the Bank

might belong to someone else. It could happen, you know.

Okay, now that you've gotten everything together and your checkbook is current, you're ready to move on to the Checkbook Balancing Worksheet.

Most bank statements have a worksheet printed on the back. I can nearly guarantee it won't be as easy to read and user-friendly as mine, but feel free to proceed with your worksheet of choice. Just fill in the blanks.

I'm going to assume you balanced to the penny the first time out. Let me be the first to offer my congratulations. Look, I of all people know what a major accomplishment this is. Feels good, doesn't it?

Now, in the off-chance your checkbook balance and bank-statement balance are not exactly the same, don't panic. Just find the error. Here are some suggestions for finding it quickly.

1. Is there an error in your addition or subtraction?
2. Did you deduct all the bank charges from your checkbook balance before you started on the worksheet?
3. Does the amount you're "out of balance" ring a bell? Does it just happen to be the exact amount of that cash advance you took last week and forgot to write down?
4. Divide the out-of-balance amount by nine. If the answer is a whole number (nothing behind the decimal point) there's a very good chance you have transposed a figure. Example: The check was for $8.59 but you wrote down $8.95 in your checkbook.
5. Did you fail to write down a deposit? (Happy find!)

If you just can't find the error, your bank will be more than happy to. Take your statement, checkbook, and worksheet to the bank with you. Leaving the mystery unsolved will only set you up for a bigger problem next month. You're going to be in a pickle if you let this go too long.

How to Prepare a Financial Statement

A financial statement is a snapshot of your financial condition at a specific point in time. It is a statement of how much you are worth in dollars after you add up your assets and deduct your liabilities or debts. I suggest you need to prepare yours once a year just to keep track of what you look like, financially speaking. Your first financial statement will be your benchmark, a reference point. Next year you will be able to compare your financial picture with this year's statement to see how you're doing. Think of it as a baseline mammogram.

If you are married, your Financial Statement should be the financial condition of Joe and Mary Average (wouldn't it be a kick if those really were your names?) as of July 1, 1996, or whatever. If single, your statement would reflect you as an individual.

The information you will need to gather is the value of your assets and the exact figure of your liabilities. Assets are anything you own of value, including cash or cash equivalents, investments, and use-assets such as your home, cars, and personal possessions of value. Debts of course are everything you owe, from credit cards to your mortgage and car loan. You'll probably have to take an inventory to gather the information you'll need for preparation of your financial statement. Don't get too detailed, however.

Cash and cash equivalents are, of course, cash, money in checking accounts and money market accounts that you could make liquid (turn into cash) in about three weeks. Investments would be stocks, bonds, mutual

PERSONAL FINANCIAL STATEMENT

Name ______________________

as of ______________________
(date)

ASSETS			
Cash and Equivalents (cash, checking & savings accounts money market accounts, etc.			
Total Cash and Cash Equivalents		+	
Investments (current net asset value of stocks, bonds, mutual funds, partnerships, etc.			
Total Investments		+	
Other Assets (current market value of real estate, automobiles, personal property, etc.)			
Total Other Assets		+	
Total Assets			+
LIABILITIES			
Liabilities (mortgages, credit card debt, personal loans, auto loans, etc.)			
Total Liabilities (Subtract from total			-
Net Worth (total assets less total liabilities)			=

funds, savings bonds, and so on, which would take longer to make liquid.

When assessing your personal property, arrive at a dollar figure for which you can reasonably sell everything you own in the next ninety days. If you have a substantial amount of jewelry, collections, or art (say a market value of over ten thousand dollars) those should be listed separately. Otherwise, come up with one figure for personal property.

Next list all your debts. Be honest and exact. If you don't know for sure, call the lender and ask. Come up with a total number for unsecured debt (credit cards, installment loans, personal loans, student loans), and another for automobile(s) and your real estate mortgage(s).

How to Develop a Spending Plan

When we were children we were accountable to grownups for just about everything from making our beds to completing homework. As we matured, little by little that accountability shifted. By the time we left home, we were no longer accountable to our parents and other authority figures; we were accountable to ourselves. Well, that's the way it's supposed to work. But the process must have a high breakdown rate because too many of us end up accountable to no one for our personal finances.

Let's see how accountable you've been to yourself with your finances. How much did you spend on food last month? Auto repairs? Credit card payments? Late fees? Cab fare? Haven't a clue or even a vague notion? Well, don't feel too badly. Most people have a difficult time coming up with anything close to exact figures for such routine expenses.

I suppose denial has something to do with it. If you have no idea what your bank balance is, it's easier to fool yourself, by adding a digit or two to the amount you think might be in there, than to face the reality of not having enough to buy a newspaper, let alone cover the cash advance you pulled out of the automatic teller machine last night.

Assuming you are sick and tired of living in a financial fog, then you should welcome the bright light that only a precise spending record will turn on in your life. I wouldn't be surprised if such clarity might be a bit intimidating. The truth is not often welcome, especially if it points out problem areas in our lives. You may be hesitant to bring into sharp focus the exact nature of your finances. Whatever your fears, please do not underestimate the value and importance of recording your spending. Knowing the truth really will set you free.

The Daily Spending Record

The first step in developing a Spending Plan is to keep a daily spending record for thirty days, or one month. This is simply a written account of money spent during a specific day. Writing it down is the only way to find out where all the money goes. If you are part of a team where one person handles the bulk of the money, this is going to require a bit of teamwork. If you have an uncooperative partner, start by becoming accountable to yourself for whatever amount of money you control. As you become more adept at managing those funds—who knows?—you might end up controlling much more; so don't underestimate the importance of adopting this invaluable new behavior.

From now on you will look at each month as having four weeks regardless of what day of the week the first falls on or how many total days are in the month: Days 1–7 will always be Week 1; Days 8–14 will always be Week 2; Days 15–21, Week 3; Days 22–End of Month, Week 4. It doesn't matter that the fourth week of every month will have anywhere from six to nine days.

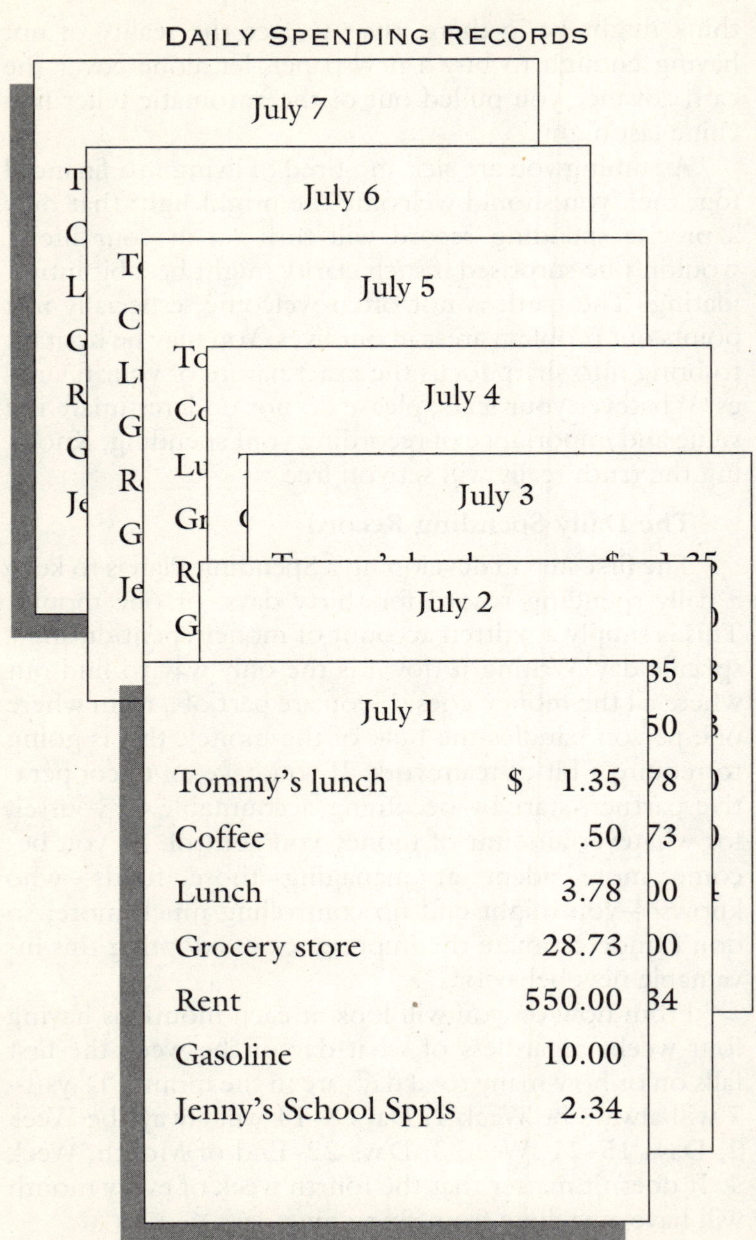
DAILY SPENDING RECORDS
July 7
July 6
July 5
July 4
July 3
July 2
July 1
Tommy's lunch $ 1.35
Coffee .50
Lunch 3.78
Grocery store 28.73
Rent 550.00
Gasoline 10.00
Jenny's School Sppls 2.34

Get yourself a little notebook or small pad of paper. Each day start with a fresh page and put the current date at the top. Each time you spend cash, make a credit card purchase (yes write it down because you've spent the money even if it doesn't feel that way), or write a check, jot down two entries: *what* and *how much*. Don't neglect writing checks into the check register too, since this spending record is not detailed as to payee and account numbers.

That's it. One page per day, every day. No time off. No endless details and no totals (for now). Given the miracle of twenty-one, this should become a habit in about three weeks.

In the case of a partnership, both you and your spouse should keep a daily spending record even if one spouse handles very little of the family income. Remember, this is not an exercise in spying on each other or making sure neither partner has any money to call their own, but simply an effort to determine where the money goes. This may not need to be a long-term activity (for some it becomes a lifelong habit), but it is certainly necessary for at least ninety days in order to develop a spending plan.

A daily spending record has a very specific purpose—to gather the information necessary to formulate a weekly spending record. Four weekly records will help you produce your first full monthly spending record.

It's the fringe benefits of this activity that are going to surprise you. If you are true to yourself and diligently write down every dollar, dime, even every penny, you spend, your spending activities are going to change dramatically simply because of this commitment to record. I don't know why. Perhaps it makes us stop spending unconsciously. Knowing you'll have to write it down makes you think twice before you drop a twenty-dollar bill on something you might otherwise have purchased in a moment of impulsiveness.

Expense categories

You have fixed expenses (car payment, rent, mortgage payment, etc.) and flexible expenses (food, gasoline, utilities, etc.). You need to come up with a list of expenses that are unique to you and your family. Try to be neither too detailed nor too general. Too many categories will be unmanageable. Too few will give you only a vague idea of where you are. The average family will likely have fifteen to twenty categories. Looking through your checkbook register or your canceled checks will help you recall expenses you have on a recurring basis.

The Weekly Spending Record

A weekly spending record is going to bring further clarity because it will summarize your daily spending activities. At the end of Week 1, gather the seven days' spending records (if you are a partnership, ideally you'll have fourteen of these; if single, just seven). Using this information, make up a simple weekly spending record similar to the illustration on the following page. This is as simple a listing as the daily records, except that it has a total spent for the week.

Average Monthly Income

Regardless of your payroll schedule or the frequency with which you receive other sources of income, next you need to come up with your average monthly income, that number which when multiplied by twelve equals your annual gross income. Note: I prefer to work with a gross figure (before any taxes or other withholding is applied), however you may be more comfortable working with a net figure, or your actual take-home pay. You decide. Just be consistent once you've made the decision. If working

WEEKLY SPENDING RECORD
Week # ________

Savings	$ 100.00
Giving	100.00
Rent	550.00
Groceries	83.46
Food (away from home)	52.73
Telephone	68.74
Gasoline	20.00
Auto maint. (oil change/lube)	14.95
Clothing	53.87
Property taxes	200.00
State & Federal taxes	250.00
School tuition	76.00
Publications	16.45
Gifts (Grandma's birthday)	9.58
Household maint. (Home Depot)	38.68
Medical	14.25
Children's misc. (school supplies)	5.86
Credit card payments	158.00
Other debt (loan payment)	75.00
Total	$1887.57

with gross, be sure to include expense categories for each of those items for which money is withheld from your wages.

Here is a simple formula for determining your average monthly income.

- Weekly: Multiply your income by 4.333
- Biweekly: Multiply your income by 2.167
- Semimonthly: Multiply your income by 2
- Quarterly: Divide your income by 3
- Annually: Divide your income by 12

When determining your average monthly income, include all sources such as salary, wages, commission, dividend and interest income, child-support payments, alimony, etc. If you get it on a regular basis, can predict its arrival, and can spend it, it's income.

The Monthly Spending Record

Once you have completed spending records for an entire month, you should transfer this information to a monthly spending record. Now the truth is coming into clear focus. Once you have totaled your entire month's spending activities, fill in your average monthly income and deduct your expenses. If you have a negative number, you must have used the credit cards quite a few times this month. This will show you how much you are overspending or underspending your income.

Keep in mind, this month will not be duplicated every month, because of irregular, intermittent, and unpredictable expenses. Repeating this process for the next two months will give you an even clearer picture.

The Monthly Spending Plan

If you are diligent and continue recording your spending, developing weekly and monthly spending records, something remarkable is bound to happen. You are going to automatically see where your problem spending lies.

I once received a letter from a lady who shared her astonishment that given her current level of spending she would spend well over $1,500 on cappuccino in the coming year. Once she started writing down her daily expenditures, it was clear that at three dollars a cup and sometimes more than once a day, this little treat was quickly destroying her solvency. She saw the big picture, determined that there were other things she'd much rather do with $1,500 each year, and made the decision on her own to make some changes. A budget would not have pointed her problem out. That's the difference between a budget and a plan. I really do detest the word *budget.*

Back to our monthly spending plan. The difference between the monthly spending record and the monthly spending plan is one little column, "Plan to Spend Next Month." Now based on what was spent in the previous month, what do you need to spend next month to make sure your expenses are less than your average monthly income? You decide. This is your spending plan, it's your life. Can you get that fast-food amount down a few notches by staying home and cooking? Anything you can do to cut that huge heating bill in half? (Yes, there are lots of things you can do.) And that entertainment category. Yikes! Is this really where you want that much money to go each month? If your situation is severe—cutting out all optionals leaves you still spending more than you earn—you may need to look at some drastic cost-cutting measures like moving into less expensive housing or selling a car. There are only three ways to change this picture: increase income, decrease expenses, or sell assets.

SAMPLE MONTHLY SPENDING RECORD

Category	Wk. 1	Wk. 2	Wk. 3	Wk. 4	Total
Savings	$ 100.00	$ 100.00	$ 100.00	$ 100.00	$ 400.00
Giving	100.00	$ 100.00	$ 100.00	$ 100.00	400.00
Rent	550.00				550.00
Groceries	83.46	237.65	58.60	74.34	454.05
Food (away)	52.73	14.50	5.76	45.85	118.84
Electricity		87.50			87.50
Heating fuel					00.00
Telephone	68.74				68.74
Car payments			279.00	183.00	462.00
Gasoline	20.00	20.00	20.00	20.00	80.00
Auto maint.	14.95		37.50		52.45
Insurance		72.50		22.00	94.50
Clothing	53.87	89.00		12.98	155.85
Property taxes	200.00				200.00
St. & Fed. taxes	250.00		250.00		500.00
School tuition	76.00				76.00
Publications	14.70				14.70
Gifts	9.58				9.58
Entertainment		25.00		10.50	35.50
Haircuts				17.50	17.50
House maint.	38.68	21.53	15.67		75.88
Medical	14.25				14.25
Children's misc.	5.86		24.00	10.00	39.86
Credit cards	158.00				158.00
Other debt	75.00				75.00
Miscellaneous					
Totals	**$1,887.57**	**772.68**	**915.53**	**606.17**	**$4180.20**

Monthly Spending Plan

Month of ______

Category	Wk. 1	Wk. 2	Wk. 3	Wk. 4	Total Spent	Plan to spend
Totals						

______ Average Monthly Income

______ Less Total Actually Spent This Month

______ Amount Underspent or <Overspent>

Amount overspent $______ ÷ Income $______ = % reduction required next month to balance.

And so you plan for the coming month. On the form for the next month, you fill in the "Plan to Spend" column ahead of time. As the weeks unfold and you fill in the actual spending, all kinds of lights are going to come on. You'll start projecting what will happen at the end of the month if you keep spending the way you did in month one. This is called managing your money, and in time it's going to feel really good. This is how to start taking control of your money instead of letting it control you.

Cash-Flow Statement

Once you have Monthly Spending Plans completed for a full year, you have the information necessary to prepare your first Cash-Flow Statement. This is a report that shows all the income for the year and all the outgo. What came in and what happened to it? Businesses rely heavily on cash-flow statements in projecting growth and boosting profits. You are no less important than a business, so an annual cash-flow statement will become a valuable tool as you better manage your money.

Using the information from your twelve monthly records, fill in the cash-flow form, which is divided into three categories: Income, Fixed Expenses, and Variable Expenses. Ideally, your exact income should equal your exact outgo. Don't panic if you can't be that exact. The fact that you've come this far is remarkable. Besides, I don't know anyone who could be precise to the penny over an entire year. It's a fine goal, so keep reaching for it.

QUICK TIPS:

1. Keep a daily spending record. Write down *what* and *how much* each time you spend money.
2. Keep a ledger to track your savings account, emergency fund, and investments.

3. Begin a New Year's tradition: Prepare a new Financial Statement on January 1 for the previous year and set specific written goals for the coming year.

Value:
Knowing my exact financial condition lifts the fog and allows me to focus on my financial goals.

CASH-FLOW STATEMENT

for ______________________________

as of ______________________

INCOME		
Gross Salaries		
Dividend Income		
Interest Income		
Savings		
Other		
Total Income		*$
OUTGO		
Savings		
Giving		
Investments		
Taxes		
Mortgage Payments		
Debt Payments		
Insurance Premiums		
Food		
Transportation		
Clothing/Personal Care		
Entertainment/Vacations		
Medical/Dental		
Utilities/Household Expenses		
Miscellaneous		
Total Outgo		*$

*These numbers should be equal

THIRTEEN

The Financially Confident Woman Gets What She Pays For

Your objective is to reeducate sellers, teach them that your money isn't theirs without your consent. If they've cheated to get your money, don't let them keep it.

DONNA MCCROHAN

It was brilliant. There's no other way to describe the way syndicated talk-show radio host Rich Buhler[1] ended a particularly difficult call, *"Just remember this: Always remain a fragrance, never become an odor."* Over the years, that little piece of advice has stuck with me like a major case of static cling.

When I was growing up I didn't fully understand the concept although I was rebuked again and again for "your attitude," "that tone of voice!" and "it's not what you say, but the way you say it." As motherhood was thrust upon me—you know, that time in life when you start saying the things your parents said—I came into full awareness of this concept.

1. Host of the radio show "Table Talk."

It's not necessarily what we say, but the way we say it. One version leaves a fragrance, the other projects an odor. Fragrance leave us yearning for more while odors send us running for cover. Time and again since first considering this fragrance/odor thing, I've been able to look back and determine what went wrong—where the negotiations broke down. It wasn't what I said to my parents that was particularly offensive but the way I said it.

Personality traits that I label as enthusiasm and zeal can easily be misconstrued as criticism and control. What I say can be taken in the wrong way. When that happens I'm afraid I give off an "odor" that does absolutely nothing to endear me to the person with whom I'm dealing. But somehow, this idea that I might be spewing forth an offending "odor" has a way of engaging my pause button, which gives me a moment to catch my breath so I can quickly reevaluate and hopefully soften up a little bit. And so it is with this whole subject of getting what you pay for. If you know how to behave with fragrance, charm, and dignity, you'll get the results you deserve every time.

Your Reasonable Expectations Should Be Met

Contrary to what the old rock and roll song stated about getting satisfaction, I believe that with the right attitude, the correct information, and reliable resources, it is possible to be satisfied with your purchase of goods and services. It's all a matter of knowing what to say and how to say it.

As consumers in this great country, we have the right to expect quality products and services at fair prices. We have the right to receive what we pay for and for sellers to stand behind their products if a problem develops.

When you think about it, it's not exactly unreasonable to expect to get what you pay for. We the faithful consumers are a necessary part of this country's economy. And as responsible stewards of the many resources entrusted to us by God, I believe we have an obligation to make sure we get what we pay for.

Confrontation has never been high on my things-I-love-to-do list. Even when I purchase something that turns out to be clearly defective I worry that the store owner won't agree with me or won't believe me and will insist the product was fine when it left the store, so I must have caused the damage. And the idea of returning an item simply because the color turns out to be wrong or I just changed my mind intimidates me beyond belief. Somewhere down inside I just don't want to give the sales clerk an opportunity to yell at me or announce over the loud speaker to the entire community that some woman up here has the unmitigated gall to change her mind.

This particular aversion has cost me a lot of money over the years. My compulsive nature and propensity to buy everything in sight, particularly if it was on sale (which for a shopaholic always confirms God's blessing on the purchase and His providential supplying of need), coupled with my fear of returning was a deadly combination of behaviors. At this point in my life I'd just as soon not know how many brand-new items—some defective, some not—I've given away or thrown out simply because I was too embarrassed, too lazy, or just couldn't be bothered to take them back.

The good news is that most sellers make a concerted effort to settle customer complaints in a satisfactory manner. Many even go beyond the minimum required by federal consumer-protection laws not only because it's the right thing to do but because it's a great way to keep us as loyal, returning customers.

But guess what? I observed the way financially responsible women live; and through mimicking their behaviors in this area of making sure I always get what I pay for, I've changed. I've learned how to practice this habit of reasonable expectation—not with a demanding demeanor or threatening attitude but just a gentle expectation that sellers are not entitled to my money without my full consent.

The more I exercise this new behavior, the more cautious I become at the point of purchase. I make selections more carefully, think things through, and actually take time to make decisions. Because I know the consequences of an inappropriate purchase may include the dreaded return to the store for refund or acceptable adjustment, making the best decision the first time around has become much more important than it used to be.

A Short History of Consumer Protection

In the late 1800s, increased industrialization in this country contributed to the opportunity for many new kinds of businesses to advertise and sell their products nationwide. As you can well imagine, along with this unprecedented growth of business came the issue of consumer problems. It was in 1938 when over one hundred people died after using a new liquid sulfa drug, a law[2] was enacted requiring manufacturers to prove the safety of new drugs to the Federal Drug Administration before putting them on the market.

World War II diverted attention from the growing lack of consumer protection. The issue didn't attract interest again until the 1960s. During that decade new programs to protect the public were put into action and existing programs were improved. In 1967 the Consumer Federation of America was formed to serve as an um-

2. Federal Food, Drug, and Cosmetic Act of 1938

brella organization of consumer, cooperative, and labor groups.

About this time Ralph Nader's book, *Unsafe at Any Speed,* was published, and he quickly emerged as the leader of a wide range of reform efforts. Many young people volunteered to work in his organization, and under his leadership they participated in research, writing, and lobbying to improve consumer protection.

During the 1960s and 1970s many new laws were enacted to protect consumers. Among them were the Motor Vehicle Safety Act (1966), the Truth in Lending Act (1969), the Consumer Product Safety Act (1972), the Toy Safety Act (1969), and legislation to strengthen the Federal Trade Commission.

Even with the rise in consumer protectionism and awareness, too many of us seem to accept that time is more important than money—that it's better to be cheated out of a few bucks or more than to waste time going after it. Most of us, if we complain at all, do so to friends and neighbors but usually let the guilty company off the hook because it's simply not worth the bother. According to Technical Assistance Research Programs only 4 percent of us let a business know when we're dissatisfied with its product or service.[3]

A new awareness in consumer rights has emerged in the past few years. Consumers of the 1990s, having been hit broadside by the recession and new trends toward frugality, have become much more anxious to exercise their rights to fairness.

Complaining with Fragrance

Probably the most important part of getting what you pay for is to keep your receipts in some kind of an

3. Donna McCrohan, *Get What You Pay for or Don't Pay at All* (New York: Crown Trade Paperbacks, 1994), 7.

organized fashion. It's not as difficult as you might imagine. Any method will do, provided you can easily put your hands on the receipt you need. If something you purchased came with an owner's manual or paperwork, staple the receipt to the front. Always take a moment to write on the receipt a brief description of the item since many receipts carry only a stock number or abbreviation that may be completely indecipherable six months from now. Receipts should be kept for at least a year, and longer for goods or services that have a reasonable life expectancy of a longer period of time.

Think of the problem-resolution process as a pyramid with a set of ascending stairs. Most problems are readily resolved at ground level where the pyramid is the largest. Some situations may require you to climb up a step or two, while more difficult situations may require going much closer to the top. However, the times you will have to climb even close to the top of the pyramid will likely be few.

When dealing with a salesperson or representative, always bear in mind that person deserves your highest respect. He or she has the right to be treated as a person with intelligence and feelings, as a person who may very well be working under difficult conditions with an unreasonable supervisor, or as a person who occasionally has a bad day just as you do.

Next, always deal reasonably and don't be rude. Consider that this stranger with whom you are dealing may very well be the visitor sitting beside you in church next Sunday!

Before beginning the complaint-resolution process, have the following things clear in your mind.

1. The exact nature of the problem.
2. Specifically how you wish it to be remedied.
3. A specific time frame in which you expect the problem will be completely solved.

4. Your next step if you are unable to find resolution at this level.

Principle: Take care of problems before leaving the store or while the service person or contractor is still on the job. Perhaps you discover before leaving the restaurant that the waitress has made a mathematical error in your bill, or the painter missed a section of baseboard in the hall bathroom. Whatever the problem, gently take care of it prior to making full payment. Remember you have a right to only pay for what you get.

Principle: Approach the highest-ranking employee with your problem, and with great dignity and grace seek satisfactory resolution. If this doesn't work, ask for the name and location of the regional manager or a phone number for customer service. Record the name and title of the person with whom you've been dealing along with the date of this confrontation. Hint: When approaching in person, be careful of how you're dressed. As unfair as it might be, people do make snap judgments based on appearance. This alone might influence what they believe to be the value in keeping you as a customer, to say nothing of the legitimacy of your problem. This is not the time to look like a mess.

Principle: The next level is the telephone call. Before you make the call, rehearse the facts of your situation. Don't dump on the receptionist. Try to speak with the highest-ranking person at this location. If you are not successful at this level, take the name and title of the person(s) with whom you spoke and record them along with the date. If you're successful in having your complaint resolved, ask that the resolution be put in writing and mailed to you. If this is not forthcoming, follow up with your own letter outlining your understanding of the terms of the agreement and a summary of the conversation.

Principle: If your complaint has not been resolved by now, a letter is your next course of action. Letters are great because you get an opportunity to collect your thoughts and arrange them orderly and logically. You have a record of what you've "said" and no one can interrupt. Be sure to include a clear and simple statement of the problem, how you've attempted resolution to date, the resolution you expect, and the date by which you expect it to be accomplished. A typed or computer-printed letter is preferable, however a neatly handwritten letter can be just as effective.

In the letter include your name, address, and daytime phone number. Make your letter brief and to the point. Include all important facts about your purchase including the date and place where you made the purchase and any information you can give about the product or service, such as serial or model numbers or specific type of service. State exactly what you want done about the problem and how long you are willing to wait to get it resolved. Be reasonable. Include photocopies of all documents regarding your problem. Avoid writing an angry, sarcastic, or threatening letter. The person reading your letter probably was not responsible for your problem but may be very helpful in resolving it. Keep a copy of your letter.

I'm sitting here looking at a heavy-duty, three-hole punch I bought about a year ago. It was quite expensive, but well-needed in this office. I believe I have a reasonable expectation that this piece of equipment should last for a long time if it is not abused or used for more work than that for which it was manufactured. It broke during the first year and I find that unacceptable. Thanks to the reminder of this chapter, I intend to send the company a letter describing my situation with a request that they repair or replace the hole punch. I'll start there and hope this situation will be resolved with this one step.

About a year ago I purchased a round-trip airplane ticket. When it arrived in the mail, the envelope contained two identical tickets with identical seat assignments and identical numbering. I immediately called to point out the error only to be informed that I'd been charged for both tickets and neither was refundable. Can you believe that? A computer glitch that was not my fault should be charged to my account?

The airline was completely unreasonable. I have fragrantly fought this now for about six months. Finally, they agreed this was their error and promised they would refund the price of the duplicate ticket. Oh, I received a refund all right, but it was for only one-half the full amount. Obviously the concept of round-trip eludes this particular company. I will continue to graciously assert my position until I get a full refund. I will not pay for something I did not receive.

Whenever it's important to prove that you sent something or sent it by a certain date, invest a few extra dollars in mailing it certified or registered, return receipt requested.

Keep a good paper trail from the beginning. This means copies of everything including receipts, your letters, letters you've received, canceled checks, and so on. Copies of contemporaneous notes will be valuable as well.

If you do not receive full satisfaction, you need to seek third-party assistance. I suggest you contact your state's Consumer Protection office. You as a consumer are well protected by laws that are meant to prevent fraud and provide consumers with an advocate. See the Resources section at the end of this book for your particular state's office, address, and phone number.

Sample Letter

Your Address
Your City, State, Zip Code

Date

Appropriate Person
Company Name
Street Address
City, State, Zip Code.

Dear Sirs (or appropriate name):

Last week I purchased a (name of product including serial and model number). I made this purchase at (location, date, and other pertinent information).

Unfortunately your product (or service) has not performed satisfactorily because (describe problem with product or service). I would appreciate your (state specific action you desire).

Enclosed are copies of my records (receipts, guarantees, warranties, canceled checks, contracts, and any other necessary documentation).

I am looking forward to your reply and resolution of my problem and will wait three weeks before seeking third-party assistance. Contact me at the above address or by phone at (home or office numbers).

Sincerely,
Your Name and Signature

The issue of consumer complaints and satisfaction, like anything, can be taken too far. I first learned of one particular lady on television and have since followed her through a newsletter she publishes. While her basic philosophy is exemplary (spend less, invest more), I believe she's taken this particular subject of consumer satisfaction way too far. Her diligence with money borders on obsession, to the point that she plans on at least three thousand dollars additional income per year to be derived from her complaint proceeds. She purposely purchases with complaints and refunds in mind. Her contention is that full satisfaction is impossible to achieve because she can always find something about which to complain. The secret of her "success" she proudly beams, is in making her complaint after the item has been consumed.

Personally I can't think of a better way to become good stewards of the resources we have than making sure each dollar spent is spent well. By eliminating purchasing mistakes and following up when we are truly not satisfied we will dramatically affect the bottom line of our financial statements. So be brave, become a documentation fiend, and always deal fragrantly.

Quick Tips:

1. Prepare a warranty notebook in which you keep all receipts clipped to the warranties and owner's manuals for your appliances and household items. If there's a problem, you'll have everything you need to make your claim.
2. When requesting a refund, repair, or replacement, keep track of all communications on a calendar. Summarize phone calls and send a follow-up letter. Don't give up until you are satisfied.
3. Consult *Consumer's Report Magazine* at your library when considering a major purchase.

Value:
No seller has the right to my money without my full consent.

FOURTEEN

The Financially Confident Woman Has Eyes for the Future

Grow old along with me!
The best is yet to be,
The last of life, for which the first was made.
Our times are in his hand
Who saith, "A whole I planned,
Youth shows but half; trust God; see all nor be afraid!"

ROBERT BROWNING

The habit of future thinking can be quite a challenge for those of us who tend to be spontaneous and quick decision makers. It goes against my natural bent to stop, think, calculate, compare, weigh, measure, go home and sleep on it, consider, reconsider, and consider some more—habits of women with long-term mentalities. But this new behavior can be developed. It's a matter of expanding one's thinking to include the big picture, not simply the present moment.

My heart was broken when I finished reading a letter from Betty. She related how she and her husband, both octogenarians, struggle from one day to the next—not because of physical limitations, but because of their financial disabilities. They led a very affluent lifestyle during their younger years and just assumed, along with millions of their peers, that everything would work out once they retired. Now that they are trying to exist on their social security benefits, they've had a rude awakening.

Not only must they continue making payments on their home because they failed to pay off their mortgage during their years of employment, they are carrying tremendous credit card debt as a result of trying to survive day by day. Their dream was that when they retired they'd travel. They would pursue hobbies and do all the things they'd put off during the years they were raising a family and building careers.

Because Betty and her husband are too old to be employed, too unemployed to qualify for more credit, too "well off" to receive public assistance, and too proud to turn to their children for help, they really have no options. I could feel the tears between the lines as she begged me to warn others of the need to prepare well for retirement. "At the time of life when we should be enjoying ourselves the most, we're sitting at a dead-end waiting to die."

Betty's letter became a personal wake-up call for Harold and me. I'll admit it: Retirement was not something on which I chose to dwell. It sounds so old! Why should we worry about it now? There will be plenty of time to prepare later, I argued. And then I was hit by this truth: *The winter season of my life will arrive on time whether I'm prepared or not.* Clearly, being prepared beats the alternative.

Planning for the future has filled me with excitement and wonder. Excitement because of all the technology and medical resources available, and wonder for why I didn't start sooner.

Outliving Your Retirement Dollars

The bad news is that increasing life expectancies means most people will outlive their retirement dollars. The good news is that running out of money is rarely a problem for the wise steward who plans ahead and anticipates retirement.

A Second Lifetime to Enjoy

We are certainly among the most fortunate in the history of the world. As American women, we can expect to live nearly one-third more years in retirement than men of the same age. And we have the knowledge and resources available to make sure we are in the best of health in order to enjoy those extra years.

If you compare yourself to your great-grandmother, you can plan to enjoy an extended life because a woman's life expectancy has nearly doubled over the last century. What an exciting prospect. It's like getting the gift of a second lifetime. But don't underestimate the fact that making your second lifetime live up to your dreams is going to take a good deal of planning, and the sooner the better.

Your Probable Life Span

Of course none of us can know how long we will live, but we can make some educated predictions based upon statistics and probabilities. Your library or insurance agent will help you locate a current ordinary mortality table, or you can use the one which follows. Using your present age, your health, and physical condition, predict how many years you will live.

Your Projected Retirement Income

The first place to start in projecting your retirement income is the Social Security Administration. You can call 1-800-772-1213 to request a Projected-Earnings Statement. This is important for several reasons:

- You'll be able to see if all your employment has been included in your SSI account.

Ordinary Mortality Table
Average Future Lifetime

AGE	MALE	FEMALE	AGE	MALE	FEMALE
0	70.83	75.83	25	47.84	52.34
1	70.13	75.04	26	46.93	51.40
2	69.20	74.11	27	46.01	50.46
3	68.27	73.17	28	45.09	49.52
4	67.43	72.23	29	44.16	48.59
5	66.40	71.28	30	43.24	47.65
6	65.46	70.34	31	42.31	46.71
7	64.52	69.39	32	41.38	45.78
8	63.57	68.44	33	40.46	44.84
9	62.62	67.48	34	39.54	43.91
10	61.66	66.53	35	38.61	42.98
11	60.71	65.58	36	37.69	42.05
12	59.75	64.62	37	36.78	41.12
13	58.80	63.67	38	35.87	40.20
14	57.86	62.71	39	34.96	39.28
15	56.93	61.76	40	34.05	38.36
16	56.00	60.82	41	33.16	37.46
17	55.09	59.87	42	32.26	36.55
18	54.18	59.93	43	31.38	35.66
19	53.27	57.98	44	30.50	34.77
20	52.37	57.04	45	29.62	33.88
21	51.47	56.10	46	28.76	33.00
22	50.57	55.16	47	27.90	32.12
23	49.66	54.22	48	27.04	31.25
24	48.75	53.28	49	26.20	30.39

AGE	MALE	FEMALE	AGE	MALE	FEMALE
50	25.36	29.53	75	8.31	10.32
51	24.52	28.67	76	7.84	9.71
52	23.70	27.82	77	7.40	9.12
53	22.89	26.98	78	6.97	8.55
54	22.08	26.14	79	6.57	8.01
55	21.29	25.31	80	6.18	7.48
56	20.51	24.49	81	5.80	6.98
57	19.74	23.67	82	5.44	6.49
58	18.99	22.86	83	5.09	6.03
59	18.24	22.05	84	4.77	5.59
60	17.51	21.25	85	4.46	5.18
61	16.79	20.44	86	4.18	4.80
62	16.08	19.65	87	3.91	4.43
63	15.38	18.86	88	3.66	4.09
64	14.70	18.08	89	3.41	3.77
65	14.04	17.32	90	3.18	3.45
66	13.39	16.57	91	2.94	3.15
67	12.76	15.83	92	2.70	2.85
68	12.14	15.10	93	2.44	2.55
69	11.54	14.38	94	2.17	2.24
70	10.96	13.67	95	1.87	1.91
71	10.39	12.97	96	1.54	1.56
72	9.84	12.28	97	1.20	1.21
73	9.30	11.60	98	.84	.84
74	8.79	10.95	99	.50	.50

- ▼ You'll have an opportunity to correct any errors (the agency seems to have a very high goof rate).
- ▼ You will be able to project your SSI if you continue contributing at your present rate.

Next you need to take a look at your present savings, investments, and other sources of income. If your investments and savings continue to grow at the current rate with no withdrawals, estimate how much of an income stream they will generate by the time you retire. Remember, you will want to withdraw interest, only if possible, to allow the principle to continue growing. If you have yet to begin saving and investing, how much will you need to reach your retirement goals?

Your Retirement Expenses

It is generally agreed that most Americans will need an income equal to at least 70 percent of their peak annual working income for each year of retirement. Now I don't wish to be a pessimist, but it is also generally accepted that we shouldn't count on Social Security benefits continuing at their present level. Clearly, we shouldn't expect SSI to provide much of our retirement nest egg.

Plan on a Long Retirement

Once you have determined the approximate annual income you'll need during retirement, work backwards and determine how much you will need to invest or save each year starting right now in order to amass the necessary sum in the years you have left to prepare.

Paying Off Your Mortgage

Have you ever wondered why the typical home mortgage has a life of twenty-five to thirty years? Ideally that's the amount of time it should take to pay one off prior to retirement. However, in current times very few mortgages are ever paid off because we move a lot and we buy into refinancing and equity loans.

I suggest we go back to the original thinking—the assumption that we will pay off our home mortgages prior to retirement. The security of knowing we have a place to live free from rent or monthly payment is a retirement gift we need to give ourselves.

A Will Is only Slightly Better Than Nothing

Most people agree that having a will is necessary. However, only 20 to 35 percent of all adults in the United States have actually signed one. In the strictest sense of the word, everyone has a will. If you haven't signed one, your state has one for you based on laws and statutes that vary from state to state.

Basically a will:

- ▼ Names your executor—the person you desire to finish your affairs and carry out the wishes in your will.
- ▼ Nominates a guardian for your minor children—the person you wish to finish raising the kids, providing them a home and personal care.

Probate Is Something to Be Avoided

Probate is a very costly court procedure necessary any time a person fails to plan ahead. Probate calls upon a judge to make sure all your taxes are paid, pay your debts from the assets of your estate, take an inventory of your estate, appraise its value and distribute it to your heirs. Probate involves many people, such as the executor, attorneys, appraisers, and court personnel who are all paid a commission—from your estate.

If you do not take preventive action, probate of your estate will likely be mandatory, unless your estate is very small. I suggest that you do anything you possibly can to avoid probate. It invades your privacy because every shred of documentation that goes through the probate process becomes public record. Probate is very expensive and could easily present a financial hardship for your spouse and heirs.

There are reasonable ways to avoid probate. While the laws and statutes are different in each state, I suggest you make this matter the subject of some personal research. Check with your public or local college library and learn all you can about lifetime gifts as a way of distributing your estate prior to your death, joint tenancy, tax-deferred annuities, and revocable living trusts.

As with all of life's important decisions, seek counsel from wise and trustworthy individuals. Take your time to make reasoned choices, and never sign or agree to anything that you do not fully understand.

With the right kind of vision for the future, you will be able to welcome the sunset of your life, excited because you've successfully saved the best for last!

Quick Tips:

1. Don't look at the 60 cents you spend each day at the soft drink machine as just 60 cents. Buy your favorite soft drink in bulk at 25 cents a can and bring your own. Look at it as saving 35 cents a day times 5 days a week, which equals $1.75 a week or $87 per year, or $2,610 over one's career.
2. Call the Social Security Administration at 1-800-772-1213 and ask for a request form. Send it in and within three weeks you'll have a printout that shows your

earnings for every year you've ever worked plus an estimate of your benefits at various retirement ages.

3. If you haven't written a will, do it now. If you have one, review it annually.

Value:
It's the little things that count and if ignored can sabotage my best financial intentions.

PART FOUR

Becoming a Financially Confident Woman

FIFTEEN

Six-Week Plan of Action

Little drops of water wear down big stones.

RUSSIAN PROVERB

Once you can do something for twenty-one consecutive repetitions, whether it's exercising, learning an instrument, or practicing new behaviors with money, you will be well on your way to establishing a new habit. Another cycle of twenty-one repetitions, or six weeks if repeated on a daily basis, will establish the new behavior as a lifelong behavior.

You will be able to take these general guidelines and apply them to your particular set of circumstances. During this six-week period you should have the opportunity to balance your checkbook twice—which will be a good start, but hardly sufficient repetition to establish that particular activity as a habit. There are many things that are not done on a daily basis but that you will want to include in your list of new habits to learn.

I am a firm believer in the value of journaling. I recommend the next six weeks include intensive writing on your part. Find a notebook or journal that you can keep in a private and secure place. A three-ring binder works well and will accommodate your journaling, spending records, and spending plans.

Spending Records

It's time to start keeping a daily spending record. Think of this as counting—counting what comes in and what goes out. The journey to financial clarity begins by simply counting. Start right away regardless of where you are in the calendar month and continue every day for the next six weeks (at the very least). Follow the instructions in chapter 11 for keeping a Daily Spending Record, Weekly Spending Reports, and the Monthly Spending Record. You will have an opportunity sometime during this time to prepare your first Monthly Spending Plan.

Week One: Choose Abstinence and Commitment

Abstinence. No, you haven't stumbled into a twelve-step recovery program. Not that I have anything against the twelve-step programs. In fact for those who have severe spending problems, Debtor's Anonymous is highly recommended.

Abstinence simply means to keep oneself back, to refrain voluntarily. Abstinence is the primary tool for getting out of debt. So for those who have unsecured debt, voluntarily abstaining from incurring any new debt for the next six weeks will be a challenge indeed. First, separate yourself from the credit cards. At the very least, move them from your wallet or purse to a place in your home where they will be secure. At the most, cancel all but one of them (it's a good idea to keep one all-purpose credit card), cut them up, and return the pieces to the issuer.

Tip: Freeze the one you choose in a container of water. Keep this credit card "safe" in your freezer. You'll know where the card is, and you'll also feel pretty silly standing there at the sink waiting for it to thaw so you can make a compulsive purchase.

Abstinence is a simple tool, but do not underestimate it. This week's focus is on not incurring debt, don't beat yourself up right now about repayment.

You may even want to devote a section of your journal to abstinence and start listing and writing about other things you will refrain from doing. Ask God to bring to your mind those habits that are hindering your journey.

Commitment. In your journal, make a written commitment to the amount of money you will begin giving and the amount you will pay to yourself. Select a savings vehicle (savings account, sugar bowl, mutual fund) into which you will deposit your savings.

Week Two: Explore Your Belief System

In your journal, write down your fundamental beliefs about money. Refer to chapter 4 to see if any of the beliefs described there strike a cord. Make a heading, "My training." Write your memories of situations involving the way money was dealt with in your family. Follow this by "My adult money beliefs." How did those events shape what you think about money today? What did each event teach you about the way you should or shouldn't think about money? You should be able to come up with three or four of these applicable memories. The more you write the sooner you'll see a connection between what you learned about money and how you behave with it today.

Answer the following questions as a way of getting in touch with your money beliefs.

1. How much money did your family have?
2. Were you poor? Rich?

3. Have you since discovered that your family was richer (or poorer) than you thought when you were a child?
4. When you really needed something as a child, who did you ask? Why?
5. When you really *wanted* something as a child, who did you ask? Why?
6. Did you have about the same, more, or less money than your childhood friends?
7. Whose job was it to earn the money for your family?
8. Whose job was it to spend the money?
9. Who made the financial decisions?
10. What false beliefs, if any, did you find in your personal search? Write about the correct and healthy beliefs you have.

These questions are meant to jump-start your memory and help you sift through all the money training you've had from your earliest recollection.

Identify false money beliefs. Write them down and commit to removing them from your life by replacing them with solid values.

Finish the week by making a fresh new list of your personal money beliefs.

Week Three: Take Stock

Values

1. Using the work you did last week in determining your money beliefs, what value(s) will become your life guide for handling money?
2. What new money attitudes will become an outward manifestation of this value(s)?

Inventory

This week prepare a written inventory of your financial matters. Here is a list of the information you need:

Your Debts. For each nonmortgage debt you have, write down the following three things about that debt:

1. What is the current total outstanding balance?
2. What is the interest rate?
3. What is the current minimum monthly payment?
4. If you continue making this minimum payment each month and incur no new debt, how many monthly payments will you have to make until the debt is completely paid?

Do some real soul searching in this exercise. Think back to debts you might have but that you've tried to forget, like that thousand bucks you borrowed from your sister five years ago. You need to pay it back. Write it down.

Your Assets. Make a list of the things you own that have a market value. Be as detailed as you want.

Week Four: Find Your Balance

By now you should have received a bank statement for your checking account. Refer to chapter 11 and balance it following those instructions. If it takes all week, so what? Cut yourself a little slack and stick with it. It *will* balance.

Prepare your Personal Financial Statement to determine your current net worth. In the event you have a negative net worth, meaning you owe more than you own, don't do anything rash. Just face the truth and commit to getting that situation reversed as soon as possible.

Week Five: Formulate a Get-Out-of-Debt Plan

Using the information from last week, make a written plan for your full debt repayment. Make a written contract with yourself as to how you plan to pay each of your debts in full. Don't be discouraged. If you do not add to your debts and begin a systematic repayment plan, full repayment will happen more quickly than you might imagine. Don't be discouraged—be excited! You've taken a major step toward financial confidence.

Week Six: Expand The Habit Calendar

You've now spent five weeks focusing on all kinds of financial issues, from paying God to paying yourself, abstaining from destructive behaviors, your money beliefs and your values, what you have, what you owe, and how long it will take to reach debt-free status. Every little financial nerve in your body is probably tingling with excitement.

So what are the habits you want to establish for the future? They don't all have to be money related. Go ahead and throw in a serious skin-care program. Write your new habits down. Now select the one on which you most want to concentrate. On your calendar, plot out the miraculous twenty-one repetitions—when you start and when this new behavior will be established as a lifelong behavior.

CONCLUSION

A Final Thought

Hard work is worthwhile, but empty talk will make you poor.

PROVERBS 14:23

Well, our time together has just about come to a close. I don't know about you, but I'm excited! In the course of writing this book, I kept beside the keyboard a pad on which I jotted down new habits I want to learn. My own belief system has been refined and enhanced. I have a lot of work ahead of me and I'm ready to get started.

No matter what your particular calling in life right now—whether you're a wife, a mother, or a professional—you're a woman both wonderful and unique.

The timing of your life, just like you, is also unique. The time was right for you to read this book; the time was right for me to write it. God has wonderful plans for both of us; and I pray that as you change and grow, you will embrace the new challenges that will present themselves and that those opportunities will develop excellence in your life like you've never known before.

Write to me and tell me about it.

Mary Hunt
P.O. Box 2135
Paramount, CA 90723

Dear Father,
hardly a day goes by that I'm not bombarded with tempting offers to conform to society's ideas of what I need to be happy. Renew my mind so that I always find my contentment and security in You, not in the false security the world offers.
Amen

Resources

In my personal quest to become educated in the matters of personal finance, I have read many, many books, newsletters, and articles on every aspect of personal money management and beginning investing. I had no idea so much wonderful information was available. Let me tell you a little about my personal reading habits.

First, I am a slow, methodical reader. I read with great expression, pausing at each comma and coming to a full and complete stop at each period. You can't imagine the sparkle and excitement I can read into the Library of Congress Cataloging-in-Publication Data at the front of every book, which, because you read my introduction, you know I always read.

Second, I have a very short attention span. Ask my husband. Perhaps that's because I have an overactive mind. A book has to be exceptional indeed to keep me turning the pages.

Third, I admit personal finance is not the most exciting subject matter. I've learned that for me, no matter how excellent the information, if it is not presented in an entertaining style, a style that holds my interest, I just can't stick with it long enough to learn anything.

Put these facts together and you will understand why a book that I have actually read, and one for which I go so far as to recommend that others do likewise, has passed quite a few rigid qualifiers.

The following resources have become permanent residents of my own library, which means I value them highly. A few have become so highlighted, underlined, and dog-eared they are living proof of my desire to wear things out.

In my opinion, these are the best of the best on how to spend less, save more, defeat compulsive behavior, get out of debt, and begin investing. I am confident you will benefit greatly from reading any of these works. I have shamelessly included my first two books in the list because, yes, they are among my favorites.

Before you make any kind of financial investment in books, however, check with your library and borrow these books. While you're there take a look at the shelves in the personal-finance section. You'll probably find dozens of excellent books I've never even heard of. And if you do? Drop me a line and let me know what you find.

Happy reading!

Books

Briles, Judith. *Money Sense.* Chicago: Moody Press, 1995.

Carroll, Ted. *Live Debt-Free.* Holbrook, Massachusetts: Bob Adams, Inc. Publishing, 1991.

Catalano, Ellen Mohr and Nina Sonenberg. *Consuming Passions, Help for Compulsive Shoppers.* Oakland, California: New Harbinger Publications, Inc., 1993.

Chilton, David. *The Wealthy Barber.* Rocklin, California: Prima Publishing, 1991.

Coleman, Sally and Nancy Hull-Mast. *Can't Buy Me Love.* Minneapolis, Minnesota: CompCare Publishers, 1992.

Cross, Wilbur. *Retirement Planning Made Simple.* New York: Doubleday, 1991.

Danenberg, Alvin H. *21 1/2 Steps to Financial Security.* Chicago: International Publishing Corporation, 1995.

Detweiler, Gerri. *The Ultimate Credit Handbook.* New York: Plume Books, 1993.

Dominguez, Joe and Vicki Robin. *Your Money or Your Life.* New York: Penguin Books, 1992.

Dunnan, Nancy. *Your First Financial Steps.* New York: HarperPerennial, 1995.

Eisenson, Marc. *The Banker's Secret.* New York: Villard, 1991.

Feinberg, Andrew. *Downsize Your Debt.* New York: Penguin Books, 1993.

Gallagher, Stephanie. *Money Secrets the Pros Don't Want You to Know.* New York: Amacom, 1995.

Humber, Wilson J. *Buying Insurance.* Chicago: Moody Press, 1994.

Hunt, Mary. *The Best of Cheapskate Monthly, Simple Tips for Living Lean in the '90s.* New York: St. Martin's Press, 1993.

Hunt, Mary. *The Cheapskate Monthly Money Makeover.* New York: St. Martin's Press, 1995 (This book contains detailed information on setting up your Rapid Debt-Repayment Plan and Freedom Account.)

McCrohan, Donna. *Get What You Pay for or Don't Pay at All.* New York: Crown Paperbacks, 1994.

Miller, Calvin. *Apples, Snakes, and Bellyaches.* Texas: Word Publishing, 1990. (Okay, you caught me. This one has nothing to do with finances, but it's so much fun to read it'll give you a much deserved break.)

Morris, Kenneth M. and Alan M. Siegel. *Guide to Understanding Personal Finance.* New York: Lightbulb Press, 1992.

Morris, Kenneth M. & Alan M. Siegel, *Guide to Understanding Money & Investing.* New York: Lightbulb Press, 1993.

Mundis, Jerrold. *How to Get Out of Debt, Stay Out of Debt & Live Prosperously.* New York: Bantam Books, 1988.

O'Connor, Karen. *When Spending Takes the Place of Feeling.* Tennessee: Thomas Nelson Publishers, 1992.

O'Neill, Barbara. *Saving On a Shoestring.* Chicago: Dearborn Financial Publishing, Inc., 1995.

Perritt, Gerald W. *Mutual Funds Made Easy!* Chicago: Dearborn Financial Publishing, Inc., 1995.

Pond, Jonathan D. *The New Century Family Money Book.* New York: Dell Publishing, 1993.

Pond, Jonathan D. *1001 Ways to Cut Your Expenses.* New York: Dell, 1991.

Quinn, Jane Bryant. *Making the Most of Your Money.* New York: Simon & Schuster, 1991.

Roberts, William. *How to Save Money on Just About Everything.* Laguna Beach, California: Strebor Publications, 1993.

Rodale Press, Editors of. *Cut Your Spending in Half.* Emmaus, Pennsylvania: Rodale Press, 1994.

Shaw, Kathryn. *Investment Clubs, A Team Approach to the Stock Market.* Chicago: Dearborn Financial Publishing, Inc., 1995.

St. James, Elaine. *Simplify Your Life—100 Ways to Slow Down and Enjoy the Things That Really Matter.* New York: Hyperion, 1994.

Wesson, Carolyn. *Women Who Shop Too Much.* New York: St. Martin's Press, 1990.

Yorkey, Mike. *Saving Money Any Way You Can.* Ann Arbor, Michigan: Servant Publications, 1994.

Credit-Reporting Agencies

At least once a year order a copy of your credit report from each of the big-three credit-reporting agencies. You need to know what's in those reports about you so that you can swiftly react to errors or someone else's damaging information. Each company has their own methods of credit reporting, and just because one is okay doesn't mean the other two will be also.

A credit history is important to establish the creditworthiness of an individual to lenders. If you are married, it is important to make sure that jointly-held credit cards and loans are reported in both your names.

TRW Credit Data Corporation
P.O. Box 2106
Allen, TX 75002
(800) 392-1122

Equifax Credit
P O Box 740241
Atlanta, GA 30374-0241
(800) 685-1111

TransUnion Corporation
P O Box 8070
North Olmsted, OH 44070-8070
(800) 851-2674

STATE CONSUMER PROTECTION OFFICES

While I hope you never have to, if you do run into a consumer problem with which you cannot receive satisfaction, give your state Consumer Protection Office a call. You'll be surprised by the help you can receive. Remember, your tax dollars keep these offices open. They're there to serve you, so let them do their job.

Alabama
Consumer Protection Division
Office of Attorney General
11 South Union Street
Montgomery, AL 36130
(205) 261-7334
(800) 392-5658

Alaska
Consumer Protection Section
Office of Attorney General
1031 West Fourth Ave., Ste 110
Anchorage, AK 99501
(907) 279-0428

Arizona
Financial Fraud Division
Office of Attorney General
1275 West Washington St.
Phoenix, AZ 85007
(800) 352-8431

Arkansas
Consumer Protection Division
201 East Markham St.
Little Rock, AR 72201
(800) 482-8982

California
Dept. of Consumer Affairs
1020 N Street
Sacramento, CA 95814
(916) 445-0660 (complaints)
(916) 445-1254 (information)

Colorado
Consumer Protection Unit
Office of Attorney General
1525 Sherman St., 3rd Floor
Denver, CO 80208
(303) 866-5167

Connecticut
Dept. of Consumer Protection
State Office Building
165 Capitol Ave.
Hartford, CT 06106
(203) 566-4999
(800) 842-2649

Delaware
Division of Consumer Affairs
Dept. of Community Affairs
820 N. French St., 4th Floor
Wilmington DE 19801
(302) 571-3250

District of Columbia
Department of Consumer and Regulatory Affairs
614 H Street, NW
Washington, DC 20001
(202) 727-7000

Florida
Department of Agriculture and Consumer Services
Division of Consumer Services
508 Mayo Building
Tallahassee, FL 32399
(800) 327-3382
(904) 488-2226

Georgia
Governor's Office of Consumer Affairs
2 Martin Luther King Dr. SE
Plaza Level—East Tower
Atlanta, GA 30334
(800) 282-5808

Hawaii
Office of Consumer Protection
Department of Commerce and Consumer Affairs
250 S. King St. Room 520
Honolulu, HI 96812
(800) 282-5808

Illinois
Governor's Office of Citizen's Assistance
20-1 West Monroe St.
Springfield, IL 62706
(800) 642-3112

Indiana
Consumer Protection Division
Office of Attorney General
219 State House
Indianapolis, IN 46204
(800) 382-5516

Iowa
Citizen's Aide/Ombudsman
515 East 12th St.
Des Moines, IA 50319
(800) 358-5510

Kansas
Consumer Protection Division
Office of Attorney General
Kansas Judicial Center 2nd Fl
Topeka, KS 66612
(800) 432-2310

Kentucky
Consumer Protection Division
Office of Attorney General
209 Saint Clair St
Frankfort, KY 40601
(800) 432-9257

Louisiana
Consumer Protection Section
Office of Attorney General
State Capitol Building
Baton Rouge, LA 70804
(504) 342-7013

Maine
Consumer and Antitrust Division
Office of Attorney General
State House Station No. 6
Augusta, ME 04333
(207) 797-8973

Maryland
Consumer Protection Division
Office of Attorney General
7 North Caliber St.
Baltimore, MD 21202
(301) 528-8662

Massachusetts
Consumer Protection Division
Department of Attorney General
1 Ashburton Pl. 19th Floor
Boston, MA 02108
(617) 727-8400

Michigan
Consumer Protection Division
Office of Attorney General
670 Law Building
Lansing, MI 48918
(517) 373-1140

Minnesota
Office of Consumer Services
Office of Attorney General
117 University Ave
St. Paul, MN 55155
(612) 296-2331

Mississippi
Consumer Protection Division
Office of Attorney General
P. O. Box 220
Jackson, MS 39205
(601) 354-6018

Missouri
Trade Offense Division
Office of Attorney General
P. O. Box 899
Jefferson City, MO 65102
(314) 751-2616
(800) 393-8222

Montana
Consumers Affairs Unit
Department of Commerce
1424 Ninth Ave
Helena, MT 59620
(406) 444-4312

Nebraska

Consumer Protection Division
Department of Justice
2115 State Capitol
Lincoln, NE 68509
(402) 471-2682

Nevada

Commissioner of Consumer Affairs
Department of Commerce
State Mail Room Complex
Las Vegas, NV 89158
(702) 486-4150

New Hampshire

Antitrust Division
Office of Attorney General
State House Annex
Concord, NH 03301
(603) 271-3641

New Jersey

Division of Consumer Affairs
1100 Raymond Blvd., Room 504
Newark, NJ 07102
(210) 648-4010

New Mexico

Consumer and Economic Crime Division
Office of Attorney General
P. O. Box 1508
Santa Fe, NM 87503
(800) 432-2070

New York

New York State Consumer Protection Board
99 Washington Ave.
Albany NY 12210
(518) 474-8583

North Carolina
Consumer Protection Section
Office of Attorney General
Dept. of Justice Building
Raleigh, NC 27602
(910) 733-7741

North Dakota
Office of Attorney General
State Capitol Building
Bismarck, ND 58505
(701) 224-2210

Ohio
Consumer Frauds and Crimes Section
Office of Attorney General
30 East Broad St.
State Office Tower, 15th Flr
Columbus, OH 43266
(800) 262-0515

Oklahoma
Assistant Attorney General for Consumer Affairs
Office of Attorney General
112 State Capitol Building
Oklahoma City, OK 73105
(405) 521-3921

Oregon
Financial Fraud Section
Department of Justice
Justice Building
Salem, OR 97310
(503) 378-4320

Pennsylvania
Bureau of Consumer Protection
Office of Attorney General
Strawberry Square, 14th Floor
Harrisburg, PA 17120
(800) 441-2555

Rhode Island
Consumer Protection Division
Department of Attorney General
72 Pine St.
Providence, RI 02903

South Carolina
Consumer Fraud and Antitrust Section
Office of Attorney General
P. O. Box 11549
Columbia, SC 29211
(803) 734-3970

South Dakota
Division of Consumer Affairs
Office of Attorney General
Anderson Building
Pierre, SD 57501
(605) 773-4400

Tennessee
Antitrust and Consumer Protection Division
Office of Attorney General
450 James Robertson Parkway
Nashville, TN 37219
(615) 741-2672

Texas
Consumer Protection Division
Office of Attorney General
Capitol Station
P. O. Box 12548
Austin, TX 78711
(512) 463-2070

Utah
Division of Consumer Protection
Dept. of Business Regulation
160 East 300 South
Salt Lake City, UT 84145
(801) 530-6601

Vermont
Public Protection Division
Office of Attorney General
109 State St.
Montpelier, VT 05602
(802) 828-3171

Virginia
Division of Consumer Counsel
Office of Attorney General
Supreme Court Building
101 North Eighth St.
Richmond, VA 23219
(804) 786-2115

Washington
Consumer and Business Fair Practices Division
Office of Attorney General
North 121 Capitol Way
Olympia, WA 98501
(206) 753-6210

West Virginia
Consumer Protection division
Office of Attorney General
812 Quarrier St. 6th Floor
Charleston, WV 25301
(800) 368-8808

Wisconsin
Office of Consumer Protection
Department of Justice
P. O. Box 7856
Madison, WI 53707
(800) 362-8189

Wyoming
Office of Attorney General
123 State Capitol Building
Cheyenne, WY 82002
(307) 777-7841

CHEAPSKATE MONTHLY

What is *Cheapskate Monthly*?

Cheapskate Monthly is a twelve-page newsletter published twelve times a year. It is dedicated to helping those who are struggling to live within their means find practical and realistic solutions to their financial problems. *Cheapskate Monthly* provides hope, encouragement, inspiration, and motivation to individuals who are committed to financially responsible and debt-free living and provides the highest quality information and resources possible in a format exclusive of paid advertising. You will find *Cheapskate Monthly* filled with tips, humor, and just plain great information to help you stretch your dollars.

Glossary of Terms

asset: Anything of value that you own.

attitude: A way of thinking or behaving based on a group of beliefs regarding the same object or subject.

automatic teller machine (ATM): An all-too convenient way to take money from one's savings or checking account any time of the day or night. Often thought of by children as a place in a wall from which Mommy gets as much money as she wants.

belief: A feeling of certainty about the meaning of something.

cash flow: Generally referred to in terms of the money that flows into your possession. If you spend more than you bring in, you have a *negative cash flow.* The goal of a financially confident woman is to always maintain a *positive cash flow,* where more comes in than goes out.

certificate of deposit (CD): An interest-bearing receipt from a bank that guarantees that upon deposit of a specific amount of money, at a specific point in time, a guaranteed amount of interest will be paid to the bearer along with the original deposit. CDs are available in a variety of denominations and for varying time periods. The longer you agree to leave your money on deposit, the greater the interest rate you will earn.

cheapskate: One who saves regularly, gives generously, and never spends more money than she has.

collateral: An asset owned by the borrower that is pledged and held by the lender pending the borrower's faithful repayment of the debt.

credit card: A small piece of plastic that has the ability to make its bearer do strange things she probably wouldn't dream of doing with cash.

credit report: A report filed by subject's name, birth date, and social security number that gives an accounting of that person's credit activities and payment history. This report will help a new lender determine the credit worthiness of the applicant. Many prospective landlords and employers look to a person's credit report to get a true picture of the applicant's character. Major companies providing these credit report services include TRW, TransUnion, and Equifax.

diversification: The practice of spreading investments among a number of investment vehicles in order to reduce risk. It's the opposite of "putting all your eggs in one basket." A mutual fund is an example of diversification because it invests in many different securities.

financial security: That point in time when you can live the lifestyle you have chosen, financed from the assets you have accumulated, without the need for additional income.

frugality: The art of cautiously spending one's money so as to always live beneath one's means.

habit: An act or practice so frequently repeated it becomes almost automatic.

Individual Retirement Account (IRA): A personal savings account specifically designated for one's retirement. Anyone who has earned income may contribute up to two thousand dollars a year to an IRA. The money placed into an IRA may be tax deductible depending on your income and participation in other retirement plans. Even if it is not, all money in your IRA account grows on a tax-deferred basis—taxed only when you begin withdrawing funds.

interest: A fee the borrower pays to the lender for the temporary use of the lender's money.

investing: Purposely exposing money to certain levels of risk so as to cause it to multiply.

liability: A financial obligation.

liquidity: The ability of an asset to be turned into cash. Your checking account is very liquid because you can draw out the cash at any time. U.S. savings bonds are quite liquid, but it takes about three weeks to receive the cash once liquidated. The equity in your home is less liquid because of the time necessary to go through the sale and actually receive cash. Great Uncle Fred's stamp collection would probably not have a high degree of liquidity.

means: Money or other wealth available to provide one's living.

mutual fund: A corporation chartered by a particular state that pools the money from shareholders and invests in a portfolio of securities. It is "mutual" because the fund is actually owned by its shareholders who pay a pro rata share of fund operating expenses and receive a pro rata share of income earned and capital gains realized.

net asset value (NAV): The current value of a mutual fund share, stock share, or bond share. The NAV of any mutual fund, stock, or bond changes daily.

net worth: The dollar value of your assets (what you own and what is owed to you) minus your liabilities (your financial obligations.)

no-load mutual fund: A mutual fund whose shares are sold without sales charges of any kind. Some no-load funds charge a small fee, usually 1 percent, for investments held less than six months.

NSF: An abbreviation for "nonsufficient funds," which means the check bounced. It is illegal to knowingly write a check when there are not sufficient funds in your account equal to the amount of the check.

prospectus: A legal document that describes the objectives of an investment, such as a mutual fund, including risks, limitations, policies, services, and fees. By law a prospectus must be furnished to all prospective investors.

purchasing: Acquiring goods and services with a plan and purpose in mind.

saving: Putting money in a safe place where it is not exposed to the risk of loss.

secured debt: A debt that is secured or guaranteed by something of value. A mortgage debt or automobile loan are examples of secured debt. If the borrower gets into trouble, the home or the car can be sold to satisfy the obligation. Also called a "safe debt."

shopping: The activity of cruising through stores and shops with a credit card, checkbook, or cash with no real purpose in mind except to find great stuff.

solvency: Having enough money to pay one's bills, debts, and obligations with some left over.

thrift: The economical management of assets and resources.

unsecured debt: A debt that is not covered by an asset that can be liquidated by the lender in case the borrower fails to repay the loan. Almost all credit or charge card accounts fit into this category.

value: Specific types of beliefs that are so important and central to one's belief system that they act as life guides.

windfall: An unexpected sum of money in any amount.